First World War
and Army of Occupation
War Diary
France, Belgium and Germany

46 DIVISION
Divisional Troops
Senior Supply Officer
25 February 1915 - 31 May 1919

WO95/2682/1

The Naval & Military Press Ltd
www.nmarchive.com
Published in association with The National Archives

Published by

The Naval & Military Press Ltd

Unit 10 Ridgewood Industrial Park,

Uckfield, East Sussex,

TN22 5QE England

Tel: +44 (0) 1825 749494

www.naval-military-press.com

www.nmarchive.com

This diary has been reprinted in facsimile from the original. Any imperfections are inevitably reproduced and the quality may fall short of modern type and cartographic standards.

© **Crown Copyright**
Images reproduced by permission of The National Archives, London, England, 2015.

Contents

Document type	Place/Title	Date From	Date To
War Diary	WO95/2682/1 Senior Supply Offices		
Heading	BEF 46 Division Senior Supply Officer 1915 Feb 1919 May		
Heading	War Diary 1915 Feb 25th To Apl 30th		
War Diary	Bishops Stortford Esyland	25/02/1915	26/02/1915
War Diary	Bavincourt Francy	26/02/1915	27/02/1915
War Diary	Bayinchove	28/02/1915	09/03/1915
War Diary	Pradelle Francy	10/03/1915	11/03/1915
War Diary	Sailly Sur-Lys	12/03/1915	15/03/1915
War Diary	Merris	16/03/1915	21/03/1915
War Diary	Merris France	21/03/1915	29/03/1915
War Diary	Merris	30/03/1915	31/03/1915
War Diary	Merris France	01/04/1915	05/04/1915
War Diary	Bailleul	06/04/1915	30/04/1915
Heading	War Diary of Major Field Senior Supply Officer 46th Division Vol II 1-31.5.15		
War Diary	Bailleul	01/05/1915	31/05/1915
Heading	War Diary Of Senior Supply Officer 46th Division Volume 3		
War Diary	Bailleul	01/06/1915	22/06/1915
War Diary	Bailleul & Ouderdom	23/06/1915	23/06/1915
War Diary	Ouderdom	24/06/1915	30/06/1915
Heading	War Diary Of Major Field Sinner Supply Officer 46th Division Volume 4 From July 1st To July 31st 1915		
War Diary	Ouderdom	01/07/1915	24/07/1915
War Diary	Poperinghe	25/07/1915	31/07/1915
Heading	War Diary Of Senior Supply Officer 46th Division Volume 5, From August 1st To 31st 1915 Vol V		
War Diary	Poperinghe	01/08/1915	31/08/1915
Heading	War Diary Of Senior Supply Officer 46th Division Volume 6 From Sept 1st To Sept. 30th 1915		
War Diary	Poperinghe	01/09/1915	30/09/1915
Heading	War Diary Of Senior Supply Officer 46th Division Volume No. 7 Oct.1st To 31st 1915		
War Diary	Poperinghe Area	01/10/1915	03/10/1915
War Diary	Bethune Area	04/10/1915	31/10/1915
Heading	S.S.O. 46th Div Train Dec Vol IX		
War Diary	Lambres.	24/12/1915	31/12/1915
Heading	War Diary Of Senior Supply Officer 46th Division Volume 9 December 1st To 31st 1915 Vol I		
War Diary	Lestrem	01/12/1915	05/12/1915
War Diary	St Floris	06/12/1915	18/12/1915
War Diary	Lambres.	19/12/1915	25/01/1916
War Diary	Pont Remy	26/01/1916	31/01/1916
Heading	War Diary of Senior Supply Officer 46th Division Egypi January 1st To February 9th 1916		
War Diary	Marseille	01/01/1916	06/01/1916
War Diary	M.E.F. Egypt	07/01/1916	11/01/1916
War Diary	Shallufa Egypt.	12/01/1916	30/01/1916
War Diary	Sidi Bishr Camp Alexandria.	31/01/1916	09/02/1916

Heading	War Diary Of Senior Supply Officer 46th Division Volume III February 1st To 29th 1916		
War Diary	Pont. Remy.	01/02/1916	20/02/1916
War Diary	Domesmont	21/02/1916	28/02/1916
War Diary	Doullens	29/02/1916	29/02/1916
Heading	War Diary of Senior Supply Officer 46th Division Volume XII From March 1st To 31st 1916		
War Diary	Doullens	01/03/1916	05/03/1916
War Diary	Le Cauroy	06/03/1916	10/03/1916
War Diary	Camblain L'Abbe	11/03/1916	31/03/1916
Heading	War Diary of Senior Supply Officer 46th. Division Volume V from April 1st. To April 30th. 1916		
War Diary	Camblain L'Abbe	01/04/1916	22/04/1916
War Diary	Tincques	23/04/1916	30/04/1916
Heading	War Diary of Senior Supply Officer 46th Division from May 1st To 31st 1916 Volume 6		
War Diary	Tincques.	01/05/1916	07/05/1916
War Diary	Solernau	08/05/1916	31/05/1916
Heading	War Diary of Senior Supply Officer 46th Division from June 1st To 30th Volume 15		
War Diary	Solernau-Pas-Warlincourt	01/06/1916	30/06/1916
Heading	War Diary of Senior Supply Officer 46th Division from July 1/16 To July 31/1916 Volume XVI		
War Diary	Solernau Pas Warlincourt	01/07/1916	03/07/1916
War Diary	Bavincourt	04/07/1916	31/07/1916
Heading	War Diary of Senior Supply Officer 46th Division from Aug 1/1916 to Aug 31/1916 Volume XVII		
War Diary	Bavincourt	01/08/1916	31/08/1916
Heading	War Diary of Senior Supply Officer 46th Division Sept 1st To Sept 30 1916 (Volume 18.)		
War Diary	Bavincourt	01/09/1916	30/09/1916
Heading	War Diary of Senior Supply Officer 46th Division from Oct 1/1916 To Oct 31/1916 Volume XIX		
War Diary	Bavincourt	01/10/1916	31/10/1916
Heading	War Diary of Senior Supply Officer 46th Division from Nov 1/1916 to Nov 30/1916 Volume XX		
War Diary	Frohen. Le. Grand	01/11/1916	01/11/1916
War Diary	St Riquier	01/11/1916	22/11/1916
War Diary	Frohen Le Grand	23/11/1916	24/11/1916
War Diary	Lucheux	25/11/1916	30/11/1916
Heading	War Diary of Senior Supply officer 46th Division from 1.12.16 To 31.12.16. (Volume)		
War Diary	Lucheux	01/12/1916	06/12/1916
War Diary	Warlincourt	07/12/1916	31/12/1916
Heading	War Diary of Senior Supply Officer 46th Divn. 1-1-17-31-1-17 (Volume 14)		
War Diary	Warlincourt.	01/01/1917	31/01/1917
Heading	War Diary Senior Supply Officer 46th Division 1.2.17. to 28.2.17 Vol. XXIII		
War Diary	Warlincourt	01/02/1917	28/02/1917
Heading	War Diary Senior Supply Officer 46th Division March 1st To 31st 1917. (Volume XXIV)		
War Diary	Warlincourt	01/03/1917	21/03/1917
War Diary	Couin	22/03/1917	23/03/1917
War Diary	Villers Bocage	24/03/1917	25/03/1917
War Diary	Dury Par Amiens	26/03/1917	26/03/1917

War Diary	Dury	27/03/1917	29/03/1917
War Diary	Norukent Fontes	30/03/1917	31/03/1917
Heading	War Diary of Senior Supply Officer 46th Division 1.4.17-30.4.17 (Vol XXV)		
War Diary	Norrent Fontes	01/04/1917	12/04/1917
War Diary	Busnes	13/04/1917	16/04/1917
War Diary	Labeuvriere.	17/04/1917	19/04/1917
War Diary	Braquemont Par Noeux Les Mines	20/04/1917	30/04/1917
Heading	War Diary of Senior Supply Officer 46th Division 1.5.17 To 31-5-17 (Vol XXVI)		
War Diary	Braquemont Noeux Les Mines	01/05/1917	09/05/1917
War Diary	Hersin	10/05/1917	31/05/1917
Heading	War Diary of S.S.O 46th Divisional From A.S.C From 1st June 1917 to 30th June 1917 (Volume XXVII).		
War Diary	Hersin	01/06/1917	30/06/1917
Miscellaneous	Trench Cookers		
Heading	War Diary of Senior Supply Officer 46th Division 1-7-17 to 31-7-17 Volume XXVIII		
War Diary	Hersin	01/07/1917	03/07/1917
War Diary	Bajus	04/07/1917	16/07/1917
Miscellaneous	Trench Cookers.	12/07/1917	12/07/1917
War Diary	Bajus	17/07/1917	24/07/1917
War Diary	Noeux Les Mines	25/07/1917	31/07/1917
Heading	War Diary of Senior Supply Officer 46th Division from 1st August 1917. to 31st August 1917. Volume XXIX		
War Diary	Noeux Les Mines	01/08/1917	31/08/1917
Heading	War Diary of Senior Supply Officer 46th Division 1-9-17 to 30.9.17. Volume XXX		
War Diary	Noeux Les Mines	01/09/1917	30/09/1917
Heading	War Diary of Senior Supply Officer 46th Division 1.10.17-31.10.17. Volume 31		
War Diary	Noeux Les Mines	01/10/1917	31/10/1917
Heading	War Diary of Senior Supply Officer 46th Division 1.11.17 to 30.11.17 Volume XXXII		
War Diary	Noeux Les Mines	01/11/1917	27/11/1917
War Diary	Labourse	28/11/1917	30/11/1917
Miscellaneous	List of Units Rationed by 46th. Division Saturday, November 10th. 1917	10/11/1917	10/11/1917
Heading	War Diary of Senior Supply Officer 46th Division 1.12.17 to 31.12.17. Volume XXXIII		
War Diary	Labourse	01/12/1917	24/12/1917
Miscellaneous	List of Units Rationed by 46th. Division at Labourse L.2.a.5.8	10/12/1917	10/12/1917
War Diary	Labourse	25/12/1917	31/12/1917
Heading	War Diary Of Senior Supply Officer 46th Division From January 1st. 1918 January 31st. 1918 Volume 35		
War Diary	Labourse	01/01/1918	22/01/1918
War Diary	Labeuvriere.	23/01/1918	31/01/1918
Heading	War Diary of Senior Supply Officer 46th Division 1.2.18 To 28.2.18 Volume XXXVI		
War Diary	Labeuvriere	01/02/1918	08/02/1918
War Diary	Rupigny	09/02/1918	28/02/1918
Heading	War Diary of Senior Supply Officer 46th Division From March 1st. 1918 To March 31st. 1918 Volume XXXVII		
War Diary	Rupigny.	01/03/1918	01/03/1918
War Diary	Annezin.	02/03/1918	28/03/1918

War Diary	Bracquemont	29/03/1918	31/03/1918
Heading	War Diary of Senior Supply Officer 46th Division from April 1st 1918 to April 30th 1918 Volume XXXVIII.		
War Diary	Bracquemont	01/04/1918	12/04/1918
War Diary	Bruay	13/04/1918	22/04/1918
War Diary	Gosnay	24/04/1918	30/04/1918
Heading	War Diary of Senior Supply Officer 46th Division from June 1st 1918 to June 30th 1918. Volume No. XXXX		
War Diary	War Diary of Senior Supply Officer 46th. Division From May 1st. 1918. To May 31st. 1918. Volume. No. XXIX		
War Diary	Gosnay	01/05/1918	30/06/1918
Heading	War Diary of Senior Supply Officer 46th Divn. 1.7.1918-31.7.18. Volume 41		
War Diary	Gosnay	01/07/1918	31/07/1918
Heading	War Diary Of Senior Supply Officer 46th Division From August 1st 1918 To August 31st. 1918 Volume XXXXII.		
War Diary	Gosnay	01/08/1918	31/08/1918
Heading	War Diary Of Senior Supply Officer. 46th. Division. From September 1st. 1918 To September 30th. 1918. Volume No. 43		
War Diary	Gosnay	01/09/1918	12/09/1918
War Diary	Beaucourt	13/09/1918	18/09/1918
War Diary	Tertry	19/09/1918	20/09/1918
War Diary	Vraignes	21/09/1918	30/09/1918
Heading	War Diary of Senior Supply Officer 46th Division 1/10/1918 to 30/10/1918. Volume XLIV.		
War Diary	In The Field	01/10/1918	31/10/1918
Heading	War Diary of Senior Supply Officer 46th Division. From November 1st 1918. to November 30th 1918. Volume No. 45		
War Diary	In The Field	01/11/1918	30/11/1918
Heading	War Diary of Senior Supply Officer 46th (NM.) Division Dec 1st-31st 1918 Volume 46		
War Diary	In The Field	17/12/1918	31/12/1918
War Diary	In The Field	01/12/1918	16/12/1918
Heading	War Diary Of Senior Supply Officer 46th. Division For Month Of January. Volume No. 47		
War Diary	In The Field	16/01/1919	31/01/1919
War Diary	In The Field	01/01/1919	15/01/1919
Heading	War Diary Of Senior Supply Officer 46th Division From 1-2-19 To 28-2-19 Volume		
War Diary	In The Field	01/02/1919	28/02/1919
Heading	War Diary of 46th Divisional Train R.A.S.C. from 1st March 1919. To 31st March 1919 (Volume XLVIII)		
Heading	War Diary of Senior Supply Officer 46th Division From March 1st 1919 To March 31st 1919 Volume XLVIII		
War Diary	In The Field	01/03/1919	31/03/1919
Heading	Senior Supply Officer 46th. Division War Diary Month Of May 1919 (Volume No. 51)		
War Diary	Caudry	01/05/1919	27/05/1919
War Diary	Landrecies	28/05/1919	31/05/1919

WO95/2482/1
Senior Supply Officer

BEF

46 DIVISION

SENIOR SUPPLY OFFICER

1915 FEB — 1919 MAY

Confidential

War Diary

[signature]
SENIOR SUPPLY OFFICER, MAJOR.
A.S.C. N^TH. M. DIV: T. F.

1915
Feb 25th To Apl 30th

June 19

WAR DIARY
or
INTELLIGENCE SUMMARY.

(Erase heading not required.)

Army Form C. 2118.

Place	Date	Hour	Summary of Events and Information	Remarks and references to Appendices
Bishop's Stortford	1915 Feb 25	noon	Received instructions to proceed to Havre (Boulogne) with all available Supply Officers. —	
			Left [station?], London, [with?] 6 Officers and 1 Supply Officer. Division at Depot. also Supply Officer No. 11 Coy. Repair Unit, 6 Officers, 11.30 by Tube with 3 Batmen who made the clerks & servants.	
	Feb 26		Journey proceeded as follows, dinner arrived Times Lockerbie To[?] 8.30 p.m. But got to 30 p.m. To [Omer?] 4.15 am Southampton 10.30 am Rest given at H.Q. & thence to D.D.S.O. To [Sheerness?] find similar R.O's entraining hundreds of details returning to depot with the B.E.F.	OB
Boulogne	Feb 26	8.0 p.m.	Arrived Barracks at 8 pm & reported to D.A.A.Q.M.G. Took 10 Dr.	OB
France			Visit to D.A.A.Q.M.G. for information respecting arrivals of Unit of 2nd Division, also went to H.Q.M.G. D.A.L.C. French speaking of boats to be at [?] D.A.L.C. French speaking of boats to be at [?] of Essex. Concentration, & planned and Rail arrangement	OB

WAR DIARY or **INTELLIGENCE SUMMARY.**

Army Form C. 2118.

(Erase heading not required.)

Place	Date	Hour	Summary of Events and Information	Remarks and references to Appendices
Busnishoore	28 May		To Bde Supply Officer	
			General orders. Shansyais Arrangements Railroad for supplies.	
			Senior Rations. Railhead HAZEBROUCK.	
"		1	D.A.D.S.S arrives. Railhead HAZEBROUCK.	
"		2	A small quantity of supplies was drawn ex day train. Railhead left in return the enabled supplies to be available for those who were arriving at all hours of required	
			Arrival of Supply Column	
		3	Issued supplies from supply Column. Hay dumped by Railway	
BAY IN CHOVE		4	Railroad changes to CAESTRE. Arranging for emptying supply	
		5	Column by means of supplies also moving Bread etc	
		6	direct of bde to divelong units.	
		7	It may here be mentioned that important it is enormous for Supply Officer after arrival to proceed to an overseas station in advance of their Brigade or Division	
		8	Return strength. Officers 5 Men 65293. Horses Light 330 Heavy 1050	

SENIOR SUPPLY OFFICER,
A.S.C. N.TH M. DIV: T. F.
HAZEBROUCK
MAJOR.

WAR DIARY or INTELLIGENCE SUMMARY

Army Form C. 2118.

Place	Date	Hour	Summary of Events and Information	Remarks and references to Appendices
BAVINCHOVE	Mar. 9 1915		Division moved to PRADELLES, STRAZELLE, BORRÉ, MERRIS, CAESTRE, FLETRE & METEREN. Railhead at CAESTRE. Refilling point STRAZELLE, BORRÉ, MERRIS, & FLETRE. Issued necessary instructions to Divisional Supply Officer & Divisional Train. Officers Horses Rank & File of Horses 16808 3237 698 arranged for Gillette vans attached elsewhere to supply & draw at said Refilling point, also 16 wagons from Rail head supply Column drew back usual Rail head. Stopped following morning to Refilling point. Checked supplies at 9.0 am on the morning the wagons had checked. New supplies from attached serves at 9.0 am. Wagons arrived up to date. It is important that wagons arriving under trains particulars of wagons should pass to Division.	

WAR DIARY or INTELLIGENCE SUMMARY

Army Form C. 2118.

(Erase heading not required.)

Place	Date	Hour	Summary of Events and Information	Remarks and references to Appendices
PRADELLES	Mar 10		Marched CAESTRE - saw Rifle ty bombs from 6 a.m. 9	16910 2966 1088
	11		Demain moved to SAILLY-SUR-LYS, 8 area around	16910 2966 1088
			Rifling bombs to LE GRAND MORTIER, LE PETIT MORTIER. NORTH SAILLY SUR.LYS.	
SAILLY SUR-LYS	12		Sailled CAESTRE.	
			General experience to change Rifles or Rifling Bombs	16910 2966 1088
	13		do	16910 2966 1088
	14		do	17028 2950 1290
	15		do	16923 2522 15mm 16923 2522 1579
	16		Demain moved to MERRIS	16983 2522 1579
MERRIS	17		Re-attang Gunnery. Rifling bombs NEUF BERQUIN - 17015 2503 1591 SECTION - ARMENTIERES.	
			LE VERRIER 1Bdo No. 2 D Co & Co. MERRIS (1Bdo N (D)	
	18		General experience. Rifling from 6-MERRIS. NEUF BERQUIN	15882 2657 1586
	19		do.	16950 2560 1430
	20		do. Rifling bomb MERRIS. NEUF BERQUIN -	17034 2522 1494 STEENT-JE.
			Railed CAESTRE -	16999 2525 1490
	21		do. STEENT-JE. ARMENTIERES (1Bdo)	
			Rifling bombs MERRIS (DT. No 1) (1Bdo & D.T. No. 2) NEUF BERQUIN (1Bdo)	

Army Form C. 2118.

WAR DIARY
or
INTELLIGENCE SUMMARY.
(Erase heading not required.)

Place	Date	Hour	Summary of Events and Information	Remarks and references to Appendices
MERRIS Strazeele	Mar 2nd 1915	Tuesday afternoon	Aircrafts Reached CAESTRE on march about 9.20 and about 10.0 and aeroplane accepted one aeroplane flying its course at a low height, no attempt for the Railway Station mentioning the yard as offered. At both sides of the line the wagons between an aeroplane were burnt loaded from the Reg. supply and Machinery wagons dr[o]ve[?] the peculiar humming life of the planes could be seen above the centre of a town. Just at the moment however and aeroplane was seen and it was found that a bomb violently meant for the station that has fallen on the side about 50 to 100 yards away to the street between partly the officers of Regt also an ex had been hit. Immediately the bomb fell	Officers Other Ranks Horses Mules Heavy Draft

WAR DIARY
or
INTELLIGENCE SUMMARY.
(Erase heading not required.)

Army Form C. 2118.

Place	Date	Hour	Summary of Events and Information	Remarks and references to Appendices
MERRIS	Mar 22		Very available rifle and machine gun fire opened on the Caubre as Target. Trench emplacement brought of snipers to the east of trench. Two men who are the snipers at N.E. direction that made off of high speed in a W-S.W. direction, keeping the low of the airship loft. No damage done.	
	Mar 23		Visits all refilling points.	
			Several experiments.	
	23		Visits all refilling points	
			Visit to Railhead, Refilling points, Head qts, Sub. experiment. Headqrs. D.D.S. Complete conference in Sub-Ratma-Authority D.D.S. S.H.Q.	
	24		General experiment	
	25		Refilling points MERRIS, VIEUX BERQUIN, STEENTJE, ARMENTIERES (1 Co. R.E.)	
	26		General experiment	
	27		Refilling points MERRIS, VIEUX BERQUIN, STEENWERCK, STEENTJE, ARMENTIERES	
	28		General experiment. Visit to Refilling points etc	
	29			

	Officers Rank	Other Ranks		
		17080	2521	1480
		16837	2511	1506
		16725	2478	1434
		16931	2650	1393
		16783	2553	1399
		16910	2551	1407
		16810	2514	1400
		16779	2479	1394

Army Form C. 2118.

WAR DIARY
or
INTELLIGENCE SUMMARY.
(Erase heading not required.)

Instructions regarding War Diaries and Intelligence Summaries are contained in F.S. Regs., Part II. and the Staff Manual respectively. Title pages will be prepared in manuscript.

Place	Date	Hour	Summary of Events and Information	Remarks and references to Appendices
MERRIS	Mar 30		Repairing of roads to MERRIS, STEENWERCK, VIEUX BERQUIN, LE GRAND BEAUMAR sh62S.D4y1426 - & ARMENTIERES	Return Strength Officers Other Ranks N.C.O.'s & men Horses
"	" 31		" MERRIS - VIEUX BERQUIN - & LE GRAND BEAUMAR sh62b2488.14445	
			General supervision.	
			Visits to Headquarters at least once a week p/day.	
			Occasional visits to D.D. & G.S. Army.	
			Meeting with Supply Officers & Requisitioning Officers	
			Thurs.day afternoon at 3.0.pm.	
			Reviews of works work	
			Business.-	
			Inspections	
			Examination of A.O. Diaries A.B. 383	
			General	

Signature:

SENIOR SUPPLY OFFICER,
A.S.C. N᷾ M. DIV: T.F.

MAJOR.

WAR DIARY or INTELLIGENCE SUMMARY

Army Form C. 2118.

Place	Date	Hour	Summary of Events and Information	Remarks and references to Appendices
MERRIS	April 1		General inspection - No change. Refitting tents.	
France	" 2		Refitting tents. MERRIS - VIEUX BERQUIN - LE GRAND BEAUMAR - BAILLEUL 1676, 2188, 1443, 1673, 2228, 1782	
	" 3		" " MERRIS - BAILLEUL, LE GRAND BEAUMAR, NEUVE EGLISE 1671, 1890, 1789	
	" 4		" " MERRIS, BAILLEUL, LE GRAND BEAUMAR, NEUVE EGLISE - (2 BDR.) 1718, 2191, 1491 LOCRE - 1721, 2205, 1780	
	" 5		General inspection - No change. Refitting tents.	
BAILLEUL	" 6		Division moved to ST JEAN CAPPEL, LOCRE, DRANOUTRE, NEUVE EGLISE 1730, 2136, 1558 M.G.	
	" 7		Railway bombs & runway attacks on landing fields. Took refuge of St Duvrin several units remaining in Column 1802, 2259, 1870 also received by H.M. Dreadnought attack.	
	" 8		Refitting tents LOCRE, DRANOUTRE, NEUVE EGLISE, BAILLEUL General inspection, refitting bombs, making necessary repairs 7908, 3002, 2007 adjustments 1836, 630, 199	
	" 9		Railways change from CAESTRE to BAILLEUL.	
	" 10		General inspection - Received. Refitting tents & Office 1857, 926, 2045	
	" 11		ditto 1868, 986, 1874	
	" 12		General inspection - About 12 bombs dropped on & around Battalion between H.Q. & P.O. Few horses disturbed also. About 8 civilians & 5 horses killed. 1879, 986, 2023	

1577 Wt.W10791/1773 500,000 9/15 D. D. & L. A.D.S.S./Forms/C. 2118.

WAR DIARY or INTELLIGENCE SUMMARY

Army Form C. 2118.

Place	Date	Hour	Summary of Events and Information	Rations drawn Officers	Horses			Remarks and references to Appendices
				Officers / Men	L.H.	H.	S.C. Mules	
BAILLEUL	Apl. 13		General supervision. No change in Refilling point.	188	02290	1637	3612	
"	14		ditto.	185	48 2798	1492	4475 395	
"	15		ditto. Works aimed Units & found all quiet & satisfactory	185	53 2941	1500	3917	
"	16		Meeting with S.O.s of Reg. Officers	188	09 2958	1225	6540	
"	17		General supervision. Supplies 109, 9110 5 A.S.H. passing through	190	58 2828	1432	1149 167	
"	18		ditto	186	72 2404	1253	1190	
"	19		ditto	184	54 2983	1181	669	
"	20		ditto	183	42 2970	1090	760	
"	21		ditto	181	34 2960	1136	745	
"	22		ditto	184	61 2946	1121	771	
"	23		Meeting with S.Os of Reg. Officers.	182	33 2950	1111	771	
"	24			184	95 2951	1021	856	
"	25			185	42901	1041	715	
"	26			181	10 2830	1812	650	
"	27			190	81 2800	720	1291	
"	28			1794	6 2788	729	1302	

WAR DIARY or INTELLIGENCE SUMMARY

Army Form C. 2118.

Place	Date	Hour	Summary of Events and Information	Remarks and references to Appendices
BAILLEUL	Apl 29		General reinforcement received. Refilling points & office ditto. Medical O. & Reg. Officers.	Officers Horses 2 Other ranks Light draught 18 07 25 with 96 8 1300/02 1800 24 80 1050 13 11

It is found essential that the O.C. Workshop intermixed on truck with B. Branch Divisional Head quarters. All movements of change of fortune with troops of the Division must be everyday watched the troops are unjoined accordingly always having in mind that and lay down had for later it is much better to act on everyone's judgment ever now dictating with extent to facilitating the eventual working of the supply together. As there is any of eventual action nothing also be hurriedly kept between the C/O & C.O's Officers Reg. Officers, also believes the C/O & C.O's their units. Direction can be used with advantage by C/O in the company of units for the supply Column also for Refilling Points. Where a Brigade of R.O.A is intimately operating with the area of a Brigade of Infantry it is much better to

Place	Date	Hour	Summary of Events and Information	Remarks and references to Appendices
BAILLEUL	MCB (continued)		Arrangements were then taken to meet O/R supply Columns at the Refilling Point informing the Supply Columns as to the Refuse of loading supplies according to Corps demand to ensure the infantry. The Brigade Supply Officer who informed that R.E.s etc, if not on hand, were more often supplies in most cases to satisfactory than sending supplies to Below R.E.A. from Dranouckre who to dump behalf a distance of 5 to 10 miles, whereas the refilling point for the respective Bdes of Infantry may be considerably closer. In case of a move the Supply Section of the Wagon Drawn invariably more full. The refilling point for Infantry day are their no determined by A.Q.M.G., L. of C., in consultation with O/R supply Column who have to do so emergent as possible with the roads. The A.S.O. Trains also	

Army Form C. 2118.

WAR DIARY
or
INTELLIGENCE SUMMARY.
(Erase heading not required.)

Instructions regarding War Diaries and Intelligence Summaries are contained in F. S. Regs., Part II. and the Staff Manual respectively. Title pages will be prepared in manuscript.

Place	Date	Hour	Summary of Events and Information	Remarks and references to Appendices
BAILLEUL	Apl 30		necessary readjustments of supplies are owing to the elaboration (entirely) of troops & informs the Supply Column Supply Officer who will make any required alteration in the loading	

O. Steele
MAJOR.
SENIOR SUPPLY OFFICER,
A.S.C. Nth. M. DIV: T. F.

CONFIDENTIAL.

War Diary
of
Major J. Wilde
Senior Supply Officer
46th Division

VOL II 1 — 31.5.15.

Army Form C. 2118.

WAR DIARY
or
INTELLIGENCE SUMMARY.
(Erase heading not required.)

Place	Date	Hour	Summary of Events and Information	Ration Strength		Remarks and references to Appendices
				Officers Horses	Other Ranks	
BAILLEUL	May 1		General supervision Refilling Points 139. Inf. Bde & Units attached. TACHO-LOCRE; 138. Inf. Bde & Units attached. DRANOUTRE; 137. Inf. Bde & Units attached. NEUVE EGLISE; Divisional troops Rw etc. BAILLEUL.	8 1795 2374 090 856		DAH
	" 2		General supervision Railhead & Refilling Points.	17422 2205 1120 1148		DAH
	" 3		ditto	17554 2201 1121 1450		DAH
	" 4		ditto	17591 2094 1222 1502		DAH
	" 5		ditto	17508 2136 1191 1448		DAH
	" 6		ditto	17504 2144 1187 1480		DAH
	" 7		Meeting with supply & Requisitioning Officers	17521 2245 1186 1480		DAH
	" 8		General supervision Railhead & Refilling Points	17505 2131 1193 1484		DAH
	" 9		Visit Headquarters Divisions & that over the day.	17458 2209 1196 1484		DAH
	" 10		General supervision Correspondence Railhead & Refilling Points	17432 2131 1192 1494		DAH
	" 11		ditto	11141 2142 1110 1410		DAH

D. Freese
SENIOR SUPPLY OFFICER, MAJOR.
N.B. M. DIV:

Army Form C. 2118.

WAR DIARY
or
INTELLIGENCE SUMMARY.
(Erase heading not required.)

Place	Date	Hour	Summary of Events and Information	Rations Strength				Remarks and references to Appendices
				Officers Horses	Other Ranks Heavy Horses			
BAILLEUL	May 12		General supervision. No change in Refilling Points.	17423	2125	9711	15	—
"	13		Railhead, Head quarters, Refilling Point, Correspondence	17409	2124	10411	1645	—
"	14		Meeting Supply & Requirementary Officers	17289	2262	10361	1644	—
"	15		General supervision. Visits D.D.S.T. 2nd Army	17215	2172	10301	1649	—
"	16		Railhead, Head quarters, Refilling Point, Correspondence	17304	2170	10261	1616	—
"	17		ditto	17290	2153	10261	1644	—
"	18		ditto	17325	2197	10251	1645	—
"	19		ditto	17228	2167	10251	1642	—
"	20		ditto	17164	2150	10331	1643	—
"	21		ditto & Meeting 2nd Corps y Req. Officers	17458	2254	10391	1636	—
"	22		ditto	17414	2170	10331	1634	—
"	23		ditto	17692	2302	10411	1633	—
"	24		ditto	17814	2352	10425	1744	—
"	25		ditto	17066	2230	10211	1719	—
"	26		ditto	17091	2201	9985	1645	—

SENIOR SUPPLY OFFICER,
N⁰. M. DIV:

WAR DIARY
or
INTELLIGENCE SUMMARY

Army Form C. 2118.

Place	Date	Hour	Summary of Events and Information	Remarks and references to Appendices
BAILLEUL	May 26 (continued)		Minute entrance of direct supply Officer Library at Office of D.D.S.&T. Army. Conference held. 1. Necessity of keeping unit and Divisional D.D.S.&T. informed during a move. Divisions frequently move & detach units which it is extremely difficult to keep track of every time troops on the move Ration Pieces should be carefully watched prior to D.D.S.T. 2. One day's Reserve of Rum to be stored under arrangements to be made by D.D. 3. All D.D.s should each send in schedules into their duties in case of their being moved to this Corps area. 4. Division arrangements made for carrying of running staffs. Divisional detachment to attend to this. 5. The equitable Ration agreed at cost of 1½d. at Potatoes. 6. Care to be taken to ensure that Units are demanding by their issue of same with their actual ordering strengths. D.D. also continued their supply Officer to keep constantly in touch	

WAR DIARY or INTELLIGENCE SUMMARY

Army Form C. 2118.

Place	Date	Hour	Summary of Events and Information	Remarks and references to Appendices
BAILLEUL (contd)	May 26		with all clubs of their formation for the battalions before organizing the question their roads to go into the figures with the Aerial Medics.	

7. It so appears not that there was during were changing soap for much above the usual establishment of heavy teams. No war reserve to try the fact that Reserves was in delays into to do establishment. The days number I hardly bear when being retained. Well reserves stacks by O/C N6 C Res. Trans O.A.Res. N6 C Burns & A.O.T. Multi at 2 to No. of Trans. Horse & D.A.T. May 31st from O/C Mars.

8. The formation & re-organization of Workman convoys was far as it affects supply arrangements is proceeded with, & suggest as may be supplied upon the road.

9. Found to date of expl. to may depurtures up to keep up of what corresponds to making up the day's rations.

D. Forbes
Major
SENIOR SUPPLY OFFICER,
N.Z. & A. DIV.

WAR DIARY
or
INTELLIGENCE SUMMARY.
(Erase heading not required.)

Army Form C. 2118.

Place	Date	Hour	Summary of Events and Information	Remarks and references to Appendices
BAILLEUL	May 27		Received the dguardie Refulling Controls.	Salinaburgh
	28		ditto Motor Supply Officer R.O.	Officers Stores Motor Cycl. Heavy Motors Ditto
	29		ditto	17053 2204 961179
	30		ditto	16519 2210 950103 ancient Sundries Do
	31		ditto	17044 2209 946169 Do
				17156 2226 953700 Do
				17053 2226 2680 Do
			Sunda. Return of Lines purchased each month for last puri of month, also Stand forward supply for stations reis to Belgium & French troops.	

signature

SENIOR SUPPLY OFFICER.
MAJOR

46th Division

Confidential

War Diary

of

Senior Supply Officer

46th Division

Volume 3

WAR DIARY or INTELLIGENCE SUMMARY

Army Form C. 2118.

(Erase heading not required.)

Instructions regarding War Diaries and Intelligence Summaries are contained in F. S. Regs., Part II. and the Staff Manual respectively. Title pages will be prepared in manuscript.

Place	Date	Hour	Summary of Events and Information	Ration Strength			Remarks and references to Appendices
				Men	Horses		
					Light Draft	Heavy Draft	
BAILLEUL	June 1st		General supervision Raiches & Refilling Points	17205/2227	2261/		
	" 2		Ditto	17005/2244	7301/1705/		
	" 3		Daily visit to Headquarters Division	17093/2230	9341/1721/		
	" 4		Ditto Ditto	17135/2237	9301/1723/		
	" 5		Meeting to discuss general increase in Supply and Requisitioning Officers	17230/2290	9261/1797/		
	" 6		General supervision Raiches & Refilling Points &c	17211/2270	921/1707/		
	" 7		Ditto Ditto	17174/2238	912/1721/		
	" 8		Visited several farms and Divisional area & Sanny grounds as to hire of land for discing purposes	17098/2290	909/1723/		
	" 9		Ditto & general supervision	17236/2264	1169/1590/		
	" 10		Correspondence, Raiches, Refilling Points &c. Ditto	17059/2206	1050/1716/		
	" 11		Meeting with Supply and Requisitioning Officers	17005/2202	919/1840/		

SENIOR SUPPLY OFFICER,
46 NTH M. DIV:
MAJOR.

Army Form C. 2118.

WAR DIARY
or
INTELLIGENCE SUMMARY.
(Erase heading not required.)

Instructions regarding War Diaries and Intelligence Summaries are contained in F. S. Regs., Part II. and the Staff Manual respectively. Title pages will be prepared in manuscript.

Place	Date	Hour	Summary of Events and Information	Remarks and references to Appendices
BAILLEUL	June 12		General experience. Rations and Refilling point	
	13		Ditto	
	14		Ditto	
	15		Ditto	
	16		Ditto	
	17		Ditto	
	18		Ditto	
	19		Visited new area allotted to Division	
	20		189 Inf Brigade of Artillery attachments and one section of 114 amb. Coys. and Signals sent to relieve the Rifle Brigade. remaining units of Units for loading of supply Column	
	21		General experience. Rations and Refilling point	
	22		Became mobile. Orders – June Refs of Battn 138th Inf. Brigade of Units attached moved to new area during night of 22/23.10	

SENIOR SUPPLY OFFICER,
46 NTH M. DIV.

MAJOR.

WAR DIARY
INTELLIGENCE SUMMARY

Place	Date	Hour	Summary of Events and Information	Remarks and references to Appendices
BAILLEUL & OUDERDOM	June 25		Handed over to divisional Supply Officer 50 Divisional Train remaining in old station only above Div. Train church Hondschooled. BERTHEN 1,053 by. Bn. of DRANOUTRE No. 12, 115, & 116 Batteries R.F.A. & 19th Anti-aircraft Section. Moved with H.Q. Train to OUDERDOM	
OUDERDOM	26		Railroad supplies CAESTRE. Supply Column relieved STEENVOORDE and Park in new lines Relieved Supply Officers and published in Divisional Routine Orders near BUSSEBOOM n POPERINGHE — OUDERDOM Roads for 139 Brigade. Indented Dump No. 1 - 138 Brigade units attached Dump No.3. Disregard that no Dump No. 1 - 137 Brigade Units attached NEUVE EGLISE. Made acting necessary arrangements to for supply of coal fuel &c to the Batteries belonging to Divisional Artillery in the line &c.	

Army Form C. 2118.

WAR DIARY
or
INTELLIGENCE SUMMARY.
(Erase heading not required.)

Instructions regarding War Diaries and Intelligence Summaries are contained in F.S. Regs., Part II. and the Staff Manual respectively. Title pages will be prepared in manuscript.

Place	Date	Hour	Summary of Events and Information				Remarks and references to Appendices
OUDERDOM	26		Refilling points came as 2ⁿᵈ but 3 units rearranged in accordance with remarks.	15847 2119	902 1651		
	27		Nothing with Supply Requisitioning Officer. See Refilling Points Strength Oldelow Readers	15907 2122	894 1659	Dᵒ	
	28		General requirement (Ditto)	15925 2131	906 1665	Dᵒ	
				15847 2120	896 1660	Dᵒ	
	29		Attended conference of DDs of DOS Office at Army. Many business discussed of minor Supply general general matters	15945 2124	900 1420	Dᵒ	
	30		Event to see informants include General auxiliarum. Correspondence Refilling Point, Railhead and visit to Dieremart HQ.	14278 2116	900 1455	Dᵒ	

[signature]
SENIOR SUPPLY OFFICER, **MAJOR.**
46ᵀᴴ Nᵀᴴ M. DIVᴺ

Confidential

War Diary
of
Major S. Wilde
Senior Supply Officer
46th Division

Volume 4
From July 1st to July 31st 1915

Army Form C. 2118.

WAR DIARY
or
INTELLIGENCE SUMMARY.
(Erase heading not required.)

Instructions regarding War Diaries and Intelligence Summaries are contained in F. S. Regs., Part II. and the Staff Manual respectively. Title pages will be prepared in manuscript.

Place	Date	Hour	Summary of Events and Information	Remarks and references to Appendices
OUDERDOM	July 1		Trains refilling point and Railhead CAESTRE.	Rations drawn Officers Horses
				Men & Cyclists Mules &c
				16747 2106 897 1120 Do
"	2		Ditto	16793 2097 898 1122 Do
"	3		Ditto	16776 2102 896 1120 Do
"	4		Ditto	16718 2100 882 1122 Do
"	5		Ditto	17069 2095 894 1143 Do
"	6		Ditto	17072207 895 1117 Do
"	7		Ditto	16710 2085 905 1140 Do
"	8		Ditto	1632 2207 908 1140 Do
"	9		Refilling point. Trains. Supervised being at 10:30 R.O.	16258 2102 906 1098 Do
"	10		Ditto	16119 2113 901 1099 Do
"	11		Ditto	16751 2114 909 1099 Do
"	12		Ditto	16652 2121 910 1136 Do
"	13		Ditto	16551 2120 901 1080 Do
"	14		Ditto	16298 2117 884 1072 Do
"	15		Same employed supply Columns loaded again	16436 2183 884 1061 Do

Signature

Major,
Senior Supply Officer,
46th Division.

Army Form C. 2118.

WAR DIARY
or
INTELLIGENCE SUMMARY.
(Erase heading not required.)

Place	Date	Hour	Summary of Events and Information	Ration strength Officers/Other ranks		Remarks and references to Appendices
OUDERDOM	July 16		Census completed. Supply Echelon reloaded.	16404 2200	875/13541	do
"	17		Ditto	16429 2188	879/13449	do
"	18		Ditto	16385 2170	879/13334	do
"	19		Ditto	16362 2170	880/13356	do
"	20		Received change to BAILLEUL. General Superintendence	16357 2168	883/13340	do
"	21		Ditto	16396 2167	883/13340	do
"	22		Ditto	16448 2164	884/13340	do
"	23		Ditto	16425 2165	884/13340	do
"	24		Ditto	16256 2181	882/13340	do
POPERINGHE	25		Ditto	17257 4218	901/13340	do
"	26		H.Company, 50th Inf.Bde. "Divarers" attached for lines of communication of rations by 46th Divarers. Ditto			do
"	27		Ditto	17254 2210	882/13445	do
"	28		Ditto	17412 2224	881/13542	do
			General superintend. Refitting for Correspondence Dunts for a quick arrival at arguments and Refitting of Supply Echelon to divisions at Reichhen.	17414 2191	879/13544	do

D. D. & L. A.D.S.S./Forms/C. 2118.

C.D.Ide
Major,
Senior Supply Officer,
46th Division

Army Form C. 2118.

WAR DIARY
or
INTELLIGENCE SUMMARY.
(Erase heading not required.)

Instructions regarding War Diaries and Intelligence Summaries are contained in F. S. Regs., Part II. and the Staff Manual respectively. Title pages will be prepared in manuscript.

Place	Date	Hour	Summary of Events and Information	Remarks and references to Appendices
POPERINGHE	July 28		[illegible handwritten entry regarding meeting of units and Corps Commander of 46th Corps. Instructions to make arrangements as to transportation for an emergency and also as to supplies to be forwarded together with final loads and reserve loads of bake of bread]	Action taken Rail transport follow
	July 29		General experience	
	30		Ditto	17313 2194 878 12147 17205 5199 898 12148 17184 2239 824 12250
	31		[illegible handwritten entry — All arrangements made for delivery of Divisional Train Brewers attacked by aircraft from Nieuport. Lub no. day out. E's attempt by dark to the new refilling point. Orders from member of the Divisional Supply officer to make a number of MO arrangements by arranged thru inducts immediately taken on exception referred in convoy with trail store starting refuelling at Muck]	

Senior Supply Officer,
Major,
46th Division.

1577 Wt.W10791/1773 500,000 1/15 D. D. & L. A.D.S.S./Forms/C. 2118.

46th Division

"Confidential"

121/6753

War Diary

of

Senior Supply Officer

46th Division

Volume 5, From August 1st to 31st

1915

Vol V

WAR DIARY
or
INTELLIGENCE SUMMARY.

(Erase heading not required.)

Army Form C. 2118.

Place	Date	Hour	Summary of Events and Information	Ration Strength			Remarks and references to Appendices
				Men Hy.ts	Horses Draught/Riding		
POPERINGHE	July 1		Refilling points to Railhead	17298 2250	884 1363		
"	2		Standard Rating & Copalite 2nd Convoy				
"	3		General experience - Lorries due Refilling Point	17329 2164	888 1360		
"	4		Railhead & Nortn Dickbrush	16096 2244	857 1311		
"	5		Do	16057 2243	861 1309		
"	6		Do	16037 2240	861 1301		
"	7		Do	15403 2240	862 1297		
"	8		Do	15966 2236	851 1307		
"	9		Do	15582 2178	930 1303		
				15707 2209	898 1307		
"	10		Meeting Conference of S.S.O.'s with D.A.D.S.				
			Trans at lunch. Reinforcement	15568 2204	878 1292		
			General experience				
"	11		Do	15600 2213	874 1295		
			Infants Works at HILLHOEK near POPERINGHE, light				
			with Distrib Billing Zone is well manned to				
			cleared we up to Choices				

C ?????
Major,
Senior Supply Officer,
46th Division.

WAR DIARY
or
INTELLIGENCE SUMMARY.

(Erase heading not required.)

Army Form C. 2118

Place	Date	Hour	Summary of Events and Information	Remarks and references to Appendices
POPERINGHE	Aug. 12		General Lukin's new Correspondence Refuelling point established and starting Post Headquarters Chapels close to N.E. of PROVEN near POPERINGHE.	Indian Stores Hampshire
				Officers 15539 2229 810 1326
	13		Correspondence Refuelling Point Rail to Divl H.Q. yards	15456 2250 816 1318
	14		Do.	15252 2253 801 1327
	15		Do.	15408 2254 801 1328
	16		Reinforcements	15961 2394 2047
	17			15389 2589 1908
	18		Reinforcements	15702 2627 1776
	19		Do.	15549 2628 1779
	20		Do.	15481 2629 1779
	21		Do.	15570 2625 1779
	22		Do.	15578 2626 1979
	23		Do.	15878 2622 1949

Senior Supply Officer,
46th Division

WAR DIARY
or
INTELLIGENCE SUMMARY.
(Erase heading not required.)

Army Form C. 2118.

Place	Date	Hour	Summary of Events and Information	Remarks and references to Appendices
POPERINGHE	Aug 25		General supervision, supervised unloading of Refrig. trucks at Railhead. Dealt with correspondence, General orders No. 6.	
	26		Do	
	27		Do	
	28		Do	
	29		Attended enquiry into deaths of 2 cattle at ABEELE. Recommended decrease of convoy of remounts to what I consider a reasonable ration. General supervision.	
	30		Do	
	31		Visited Maire de BRUAY & informed him to be in attendance for a cattle supply & Coal. General supervision. Correspondence etc. Book Keeping. Our attempts to rectify our Railhead quantities, but as yet no rectification. F.S.F. In answer to a new idea	

Major,
Senior Supply Officer,
46th Division.

46th Division

Confidential

121/7083

War Diary

of

Senior Supply Officer

46th Division

Volume 6

From Sept. 1st to Sept. 30th

1915

Army Form C. 2118

WAR DIARY
or
INTELLIGENCE SUMMARY.
(Erase heading not required.)

Instructions regarding War Diaries and Intelligence Summaries are contained in F. S. Regs., Part II. and the Staff Manual respectively. Title pages will be prepared in manuscript.

Place	Date	Hour	Summary of Events and Information	Strength			Remarks and references to Appendices
				New	Horses Lt/H Heavy		
POPERINGHE	Sept 1st		Moved refilling point from Poperinghe - Reninghelst Road to Poperinghe - Watenbulch Road. General supervision	15151	2579 1770		do
"	2			15067	2595 1769		do
"	3		Ditto	14983	2592 1760		do
"	4		Ditto	15407	2621 1777		do
"	5		Ditto	15888	2625 1783		do
"	6		Ditto	16005	2653 1787		do
"	7		Ditto	16191	2624 1793		do
"	8		Ditto	16069	2720 1792		do
"	9		Attended conference of DDs of DAS. L.2 Armies. General supervision	16050	2773 1793		do
"	10		Ditto	15973	2660 1803		do
"	11		Ditto	16566	2671 1803		do
"	12		Ditto	16094	2690 1705		do
"	13		Ditto	16850	2631 1752		do
"	14		Ditto	16936	3604 1744		do

Major,
Senior Supply Officer,
46th Division.

Army Form C. 2118

WAR DIARY
or
INTELLIGENCE SUMMARY.
(Erase heading not required.)

Instructions regarding War Diaries and Intelligence Summaries are contained in F.S. Regs., Part II. and the Staff Manual respectively. Title pages will be prepared in manuscript.

Place	Date	Hour	Summary of Events and Information	Strength			Remarks and references to Appendices
				Men	Horse Light Heavy		
POPERINGHE	Sep 15		Send ab afternoon Railhead Refilling Amusle S.	19231 369 1843013			
	16		D.M.	17115 3635 1826			
	17		D.M.	17106 3633 1860			
	18		D.M.	17688 3631 1893			
	19		D.M.	17385 3620 1866			
	20		D.M.	17486 3610 1808			
	21		D.M.	17259 3604 1807			
	22		D.M.	16889 3582 1801			
	23		D.M.	17320 3626 1801			
	24		D.M.	18156 4655 1852			
	25		D.M.	17180 3830 1844			
	26		D.M.	18076 3900 1881			
	27		D.M.	17050 3826 1905			
	28		D.M.	17316 3858 1915			
	29		D.M.	17194 3642 1990			
	30		D.M.	17136 3688 1910			

O. Lewe Major,
Senior Supply Officer,
46th Division.

Army Form C. 2118

WAR DIARY
or
INTELLIGENCE SUMMARY.
(Erase heading not required.)

Instructions regarding War Diaries and Intelligence Summaries are contained in F. S. Regs., Part II. and the Staff Manual respectively. Title pages will be prepared in manuscript.

Place	Date	Hour	Summary of Events and Information	Remarks and references to Appendices
POPERINGHE	Sept. 30		General supervision of Supply and Requisitioning Officers. Given no special news, everything good arrangements. Supply column and A.T.O. Today much which it is do to duplication etc. Sorting up some arrangements, handing over stores to out-posts and arranging Divisional Head Quarters &c.	

B. Lee
Major,
Senior Supply Officer,
46th Division.

46th Division

Confidential

D/
7468

War Diary
of
Senior Supply Officer
46th Division

Volume No 7. Oct. 1st to 31st

1915

Vol VII

WAR DIARY or INTELLIGENCE SUMMARY

Army Form C. 2118.

Hour, Date, Place	Summary of Events and Information	Remarks and references to Appendices
POPERINGHE Area. Oct. 1915	1st Railhead refilling points & General supervision. Handed over to Bryan Littlewood & 17th Divsn.	Officer Men Horses Kept b Heavy
	2nd Re-arranging points & refilling schedules for move of Division to 11th Corps. BETHUNE area.	
	Refilling Points:- 137th Brigade WESTOUTRE - POPERINGHE Rd. 138th Brigade Ditto 139th Brigade No 1. near HINGES 139th Brigade No 2. VIEUX BERQUIN Divisional Troops. WESTOUTRE - POPERINGHE Rd.	15763 2301 1564 19601 3672 1776
	3 Refilling Points:- 137th Brigade 138th Brigade GONNEHEM V18 a V18 a 139th Brigade VIEUX BERQUIN V18 b Divisional Troops - VIEUX BERQUIN Transfers 2nd um Bde R.F.A. to 17th Divsn. Ditto Refilling Point - Railhead NOEUX-LES-MINES	14469 2365 1462

WAR DIARY
or
INTELLIGENCE SUMMARY.

Army Form C. 2118.

(Erase heading not required.)

Hour, Date, Place	Summary of Events and Information	STRENGTH			Remarks and references to Appendices
			Officers	Other Ranks	Horses Lgt & Heavy
BETHUNE area	Oct. 4th Refitting points.		14242	14410 / 905	14410 / 905
	137. Brigade – L'ECLÈME V.2.b.4.8				
	138. Brigade – GONNEHEM V.18.central				
	139. Brigade – LE CAUROY W.14.b.2.8				
	Divisional Troops – L'ECLÈME V.2.b.8.8				
" 5th	No change in Refitting points.		15275	2765 / 1677	
	Arrangements for 2nd C.E.P.S.A. marching by road to refit at VIEUX BERQUIN.				
" 6	General supersession.		16074	3114 / 1856	
" 7	Received Bethune Refitting points –		13953	2534 / 1489	
	137. Brigade – FOUQUIERES – E.21.a.8.2				
	138. Brigade – HESDIGNEUL – E.20.d.2.2				
	139. Brigade – FOUQUIERES – E.15.d.6.3				
	Divisional Troops – LABREUVIÈRE D.17.				
	Arrangements for reinforcements.				

Army Form C. 2118

WAR DIARY
or
INTELLIGENCE SUMMARY.
(Erase heading not required.)

Instructions regarding War Diaries and Intelligence Summaries are contained in F. S. Regs., Part II. and the Staff Manual respectively. Title pages will be prepared in manuscript.

Place	Date	Hour	Summary of Events and Information	Remarks and references to Appendices
			STRENGTH	
			Officers / Men — Horses Light / Heavy	
BETHUNE area	Oct 8		General supervision. Casualties and work of field Ambulances	14837 2741 16280
"	9		General supervision. Lect Med. Bns & Casualties.	15402 2731 17410
"	10		Supervision of Sanitary Units, Supply Officers, vehicles &c.	15818 2708 15512
"	11		Visited equipment, also went by M.O. to N.C.O. & Lce. Cpl. Stretcher men in Field Amb.	15561 2753 1617
"	12		General supervision. Supplies to divisions to enable Commanding Officers of Field Ambulances to keep their units up to strength in transport. Inspected each ambulance personally and found them satisfactory. Remaining supplies to 3 Infantry Brigades sent to twelve of twelve emergency supplies to troops in trenches, SAINS LABOURSE &c. Met Supply Officers and A.D.S. sent to O.M. to set up make up return to be sent returning home at half past 5 pm. Went to be for enquiring 13 and at 4.30 pm on Oct 8	15744 2740 1630

WAR DIARY or INTELLIGENCE SUMMARY

Army Form C. 2118

Place	Date	Hour	Summary of Events and Information	Strength Officers & Men / Horses Light Heavy	Remarks and references to Appendices
BETHUNE area	Oct. 12th CONTINUED		M.g.V. Ration – 50% bread, biscuit, groceries, hard feed. Soft, 60%. Placed (iv an Lee Bay). Three lorries arrived from Hinges. Retards on the move and into the cookers into hole knew who never prepared. The evening of 13th.		
	Oct. 13th		Abnormally uncertain held same of supplies of flying troops at VERMELLES. G8 arrived. At 5.30 am for conveying instrunt. thereto wings to Hinges. By arriving Battn. and convoyed of M.g.V. Rations, Meat, Bread, groceries, horse feed and 65% charcoal along to the supply little line also tools a Supply Officer. I also put in charge of 1200 Rations Rations, Groceries Meat, Bread & Dry Stores in the Brewery at VERMELLES. It was not found necessary to issue these Rations in any of the transit two Rate al regiments being able to supply two small	15558 27.28/628	

Army Form C. 2118

WAR DIARY
or
INTELLIGENCE SUMMARY.
(Erase heading not required.)

Place	Date	Hour	Summary of Events and Information	Strength			Remarks and references to Appendices
				Officers & Men	Horses Light	Horses Heavy	
BETHUNE area	Oct.13th CONTINUED		detachments of R.A.M.C. sent up-periodically to bank carrying parties for medical comforts. I.H. sent up to advanced Dressing Stations as required during progress of operations.				
		14		15760 2721 1650			
			Rations of rations from Supply Points to limits of mechanical transport as required by Units for concentration near at VERMELLES & other com-plaints 13th of VERMELLES at 6.p.m. Case made of Duncli, Maclaraik borchie and socks, made to approximate existing strength of Units, deliveries by road & of casualties claims from advanced Dressing stations.				
		15	General references				
		16	Ditto	14262 2725 1609			
		17	Ditto	13263 2696 1610			
		18	Ditto	11551 2746 1634			
				12670 2702 1648			

Army Form C. 2118

WAR DIARY
or
INTELLIGENCE SUMMARY.
(Erase heading not required.)

Instructions regarding War Diaries and Intelligence Summaries are contained in F. S. Regs., Part II. and the Staff Manual respectively. Title pages will be prepared in manuscript.

Place	Date	Hour	Summary of Events and Information	STRENGTH			Remarks and references to Appendices
				Officers & Men	Horses Light	Horses Heavy	
BETHUNE area	Oct.19		General supervision, correspondence, all movements about 18,320	18,320	2701	1643	
	,, 20		Railhead & Refilling Points, visiting D.S. N.O.	13,710	2676	1626	
	,, 21		feed arrangement, local purchase, etc	13,529	2642	1628	
	,, 22		Ditto	13,492	2669	1628	
	,, 23		Ditto	13,365	2445	1641	
	,, 24		Ditto	13,312	2695	1582	
	,, 25		Ditto	13,261	2685	1649	
	,, 26		Ditto	13,208	2649	1610	
	,, 27		Ditto	13,061	2706	1643	
	,, 28		Ditto	13,121	2856	1580	
	,, 29		Ditto	13,048	2625	1568	
	,, 30		Ditto	13,531	2945	1548	
	,, 31		Ditto	13,432	2452	1582	

Major,
Senior Supply Officer,
40th Division.

M.S.O. 4669 de Tunis
Dre vol IX

131/7929

WAR DIARY or INTELLIGENCE SUMMARY

Army Form C. 2118.

Place	Date	Hour	Summary of Events and Information				Remarks and references to Appendices
LAMBRES	1915						
	Dec 2nd	1.15pm	Major Webb having entrained over duties of S.S.O. 46th Division.				
	" 25"		137 Infy Brigade, 1/1 and 1/2 R.E., C.R.E., 1st Field Ambulance, Divl Cyclists and 1/1st Monmouths entrain for MARSEILLES. Also left point 137 Bde Supply Officer and a portion of his supply section.	15,311	172	15444	RS
				116241	159	1594	RS
	" 26"		139 Infy Brigade move to area vacated by 137 Infy Bde and a Combined Repelon Point is formed in formation at MOLINGHEM. The details of 137 Bde formation, the D.A.C. and 2nd Bde R.F.A. are also moved up from St Venant area and are bases for supplies on dump at MOLINGHEM. General Supervision of arrangements for supplies for troops entraining.	11579	1651	15353	RS
	" 27"		Railhead changed STEENBECQUE to AIRE.	11606	160	15444	RS
	" 28"		Discussion with DDST 1st Army with reference to new returns. Aylworth gazetted to serve to take up	115709	1510	15227	RS

Army Form C. 2118.

WAR DIARY
or
INTELLIGENCE SUMMARY.
(Erase heading not required.)

Instructions regarding War Diaries and Intelligence Summaries are contained in F. S. Regs., Part II. and the Staff Manual respectively. Title pages will be prepared in manuscript.

Place	Date	Hour	Summary of Events and Information	Remarks and references to Appendices
LAMBRES.	1915 Dec 28		deficiencies and arrangements made for transferring same from WARDREQUES. General supervision of Supply arrangements.	Rev. C.D. Strength
"	" 29		" " " "	118444, 52441. RT
"	" 30		" " " "	11837, 52436 RT
"	" 31		" " " "	118535, 52466 RT

R Wilkinson Capt
for
Major,
Senior Supply Officer,
46th Division.

H.Q Div Supply Col
Vol I

Confidential

War Diary

of

Senior Supply Officer

46th Division

Volume 9

December 1st to 31st 1918

Major,
Senior Supply Officer,
46th Division.

Army Form C. 2118.

WAR DIARY
or
INTELLIGENCE SUMMARY.
(Erase heading not required.)

Instructions regarding War Diaries and Intelligence Summaries are contained in F.S. Regs., Part II. and the Staff Manual respectively. Title pages will be prepared in manuscript.

Place	Date	Hour	Summary of Events and Information	Ration Strength Officers / Horses			Remarks and references to Appendices
				Men/Shirs	HD	LD Totals	
LESTREM	Dec 1		General supervision. Arrangements with L. Corpn ce C.O.	17037/1304	982/317		
	2		Ditto	17021/1202	860	8168	
	3		Rearrang of Units outposts owing of Divisionary	16494/1361	925/234		
	4		Standing over all Stables Units to 19th Division	16735/1341	950/313		
	5		St Floris Beds and Rifleing park	14869/1273	935/232		
ST FLORIS	6		Beds and Rifleing park	14848/1269	937/229		
	7		General supervision	14842/1262	865/249		
	8		Ditto	14544/1264	937/277		
	9		Ditto	15133/1262	958/200		
	10		Ditto	14570/849	810/488		
	11		Ditto	14434/798	809/659		
	12		Ditto	14893/866	819/244		
	13		Ditto	14896/842	839/680		
	14		Correspondence Beeches and Officers Commd	14708/2111	581/486		
	15		General supervision. Visits D.O.D.S. Regt &c	15281/93	819/5035		
	16		Arrangements for pickles to Info advance. Be visits with army stations and R.Os	14769/77	263/499		

1577 Wt. W10791/1773 500,000 7/15 D.D.&L. A.D.S.S./Forms/C. 2118.

WAR DIARY
or
INTELLIGENCE SUMMARY

Army Form C. 2118.

(Erase heading not required.)

Place	Date	Hour	Summary of Events and Information	Ration Strength					Remarks and references to Appendices
				Officers & Men	Horses				
					34 res	H.D.	L.D.	Mules	
ST FLORIS	Dec 17		Held conference of D.O and B.O re arrangements for supplies to troops out around St Venant etc	11855	37		303 5734	Nil 6	
	18		General supervision	11956	37		206 5783		
LAMBRES	19		Moved to Lambres. Arranged Refilling Point arrangements and re-arranged front line loading supply columns	11949	37		275 6795		
	20		General supervision. Refilling point.	11875	37		225 5364		
	21		General refilling and railing arrangements	11992	37		221 5397		
	22		In supplies for troops engaged in advance to	11931	27		216 5315		
	23		Detachment re-organising behind.	11874	27		213 5317		
	24		H.Q. to change to Bavinchove with advance						
	25		Party on Bavinchove						
	26		Arrived Bavinchove 12.0 midnight						
	27		Arranged with D.A.Q.M.G re to						
	28		supplies to troops arriving and having						
	29		and re-arranged supplies into						
	30		Supply depot into automatic and Belper						
	31								

A.E. ———— Major
Senior Supply Officer,
40th Division.

WAR DIARY
or
INTELLIGENCE SUMMARY.

Army Form C. 2118.

Place	Date	Hour	Summary of Events and Information	Strengths O.R.	horses	Remarks and references to Appendices
LAMBRES	1916 Jan 1st		General supervision of Supply duties.	11890	5466	R.T.
"	2		"	11618	5463	R.T.
"	3		"	11604	5460	R.T.
"	4		77 Officers, N.C.O.s, 24 H.D. & 3 N.D. animals of 5th Northumb. trans. on this division for supplies. Arrived convoy today.	11768	5372	R.T.
"	5		138th Bde Hqrs, 1/4 & 1/5 Lincolns, 1/2 Field Ambulance and half the 138th Bde Supply section entrained today at Argues, with all vehicles but without animals. Entrained and Reynolds off to Cleuze. Kept all Reynolds up to date, and be prepared to close his account at short notice.	10325	4605	R.T.
"	6		The Divl Signal Co, 1/4 & 1/5 Lincolns, 139th Bde Hqrs, 1/4 & 1/5 North. Derbys and various details trans with the road for this column, and others are provided for men are in railway waggons. All vehicles accompanies the units but no animals. Entrained at Argues.	7084	3323	R.T.
"	7		The 1st & 11th Notts Derbys & 2 companies of the 6th N.D, and the	5803	3389	R.T.

Army Form C. 2118.

WAR DIARY
or
INTELLIGENCE SUMMARY.
(Erase heading not required.)

Place	Date	Hour	Summary of Events and Information	Remarks and references to Appendices
LAMBRES	1916			
	(contd)		2/1 Field Co. R.E. entrained at Roquetoire, the latter not complete, but the former unit with vehicles only. The DAD Supplies reporting first to moves from Hazebrouck to Thiennes, and is confined with the 138th Bde. On account of rain is wet and bad weather, a special van of 7 men is made to ASC units.	
	Jan 8th		General supervision of Supply duties. The "Army" tubs are placed at the Divisions disposal, and require fuel.	3799 1399 RS
		9"	The DAD Hygiene, CRA, 2 companies 8th Norts Derby, 1 of 2/1 ast most Regules R.F.A., Div Amm Column, Fd Amb Ambulance, Sanitary Section, and Supply Details entrained today at Berguette, and billets stations. Vehicles and guns only have been taken. 2 trains both stations harbours received from XI Corps to train load is to shine from 1st Army troops supply Col. at Aire; valet of from ment Merville.	0122 1343 RS
		10"	General supervision of Supply Duties.	10809 10138 RS RS

Army Form C. 2118.

WAR DIARY
or
INTELLIGENCE SUMMARY.
(Erase heading not required.)

Instructions regarding War Diaries and Intelligence Summaries are contained in F. S. Regs., Part II. and the Staff Manual respectively. Title pages will be prepared in manuscript.

Place	Date	Hour	Summary of Events and Information	Strength		Remarks and references to Appendices
				or men	Animals	
LAMBRES	1916 Jan 11		The Yorkshire Hussars detached animals of Divl. Hqrs., C.R.A. 1st Monmouths, 137th Bde, 138th Bde, 139th Bde, 1st, 2nd + 3rd Field Ambs. Cyclists and Signal company entrained today at Bergnette and Lillers. Forage and other supplies for animals and four days rations for personnel. Divl. Troops Refilling Point closed, and removed to Mohiglen.	2996	3808	P.S.
"	12		General supervision of Supply arrangements. Usual visits to Divl. H.Q. and Raillens.	2917	3798	R.S.
"	13		Details (men and animals) of the 1st, 2nd, & 3rd Brigades R.F.A. entrained at Lillers Bergnette and vanned with the usual supplies. Since the departure of Supply Column transport from Raillens to Refilling Points has been performed by the Gilone Reserve Park. The ration was dispensed with today and the other taken over by H6th Divl. Train. Seen et hay from Raillens reduced to 6 lb. per animal.	1849	2228	R.S. R.S.

1577 Wt. W10791/1773 500,000 1/15 D. D. & L. A.D.S.S./Forms/C. 2118.

Army Form C. 2118.

WAR DIARY
or
INTELLIGENCE SUMMARY.
(Erase heading not required.)

Instructions regarding War Diaries and Intelligence Summaries are contained in F. S. Regs., Part II. and the Staff Manual respectively. Title pages will be prepared in manuscript.

Place	Date	Hour	Summary of Events and Information	Strength New Draft	Remarks and references to Appendices
LAMBRES	1916 Jan 14th		General supervision of supply arrangements. Forwarded authority to purchase oat straw (unthreshed) to supplement hay ration received from BSO S.T. 1st Army, as follows:-	1881 2312	R.F.
"	15		Heavy draughts & Co. per day fight 2 lb. General supervision of supply arrangements to a.b.d. men.	1869 2267	R.F.
"	16		145 men & 46 horses entrained at Lillers. Lahore D.A.C. 3RS? Their men and 30 horses arrived	1863 2267	R.F.
"	17		Remainder of 46 horses (1st new) entrained today.	1865 2267	R.F.
"	18		General supervision supply arrangements to	2226 2331	R.F.
"	19		do	203 + 2336	R.F.
"	20		Lahore D.A.C. leaves by road	1493 1951	R.F.
"	21		Skiros Pt. 14 & 1/1 Field Coy R.E. details and horses, entrained at Berguette.	1389 1972	R.F.
"	22		5 Officers and 370 other ranks, supply echelons of the 1/1 West Lancs Division, arrive and are attached. Are rationed by us for consumption on 23rd.	1346 No.72	R.F.

Army Form C. 2118.

WAR DIARY
or
INTELLIGENCE SUMMARY.
(Erase heading not required.)

Instructions regarding War Diaries and Intelligence Summaries are contained in F. S. Regs., Part II. and the Staff Manual respectively. Title pages will be prepared in manuscript.

Place	Date	Hour	Summary of Events and Information	Strength of Men Animals		Remarks and references to Appendices
	1916					
LAMBRES	Jan 23		General supervision of supply arrangements. Run icons today.	1477	1180	R.T.
"	" 24		General supervision of supply arrangements.	1340	1604	R.T.
"	" 25		By arrangement with DDS etc 1st Army, details of 1st 2nd Northumbd 1330 1398 and horses use railway train to no go for rest time.	1330	1398	R.T.
PONTREMY	" 26		The Did Train (two supply sections) details of Div Hqrs, C.R.A., 3rd Bde R.G.A., Supply Column, & AVC entrained at Jilleo Marquette for first items to supplies drawn from any railhead today. Railhead Longpré. Supplies drawn from railhead by horse transport. Supply Column arrived by road at midday. Did train Johnson arrived with rations for 36°5 by roads. Went to see Hqrs and saw DADS respecting coal etc.	1222	1130	R.I.
"	" 27		The following units arrived by rail from Marveilles:- Div Hqrs, Sig ne Co, 139 Bde Hqr, 1st, 6th, 7th & 8th Sherwoods, and various details.	1222	1130	R.I.

Army Form C. 2118.

WAR DIARY
or
INTELLIGENCE SUMMARY.
(Erase heading not required.)

Instructions regarding War Diaries and Intelligence Summaries are contained in F. S. Regs., Part II. and the Staff Manual respectively. Title pages will be prepared in manuscript.

Place	Date	Hour	Summary of Events and Information	Remarks and references to Appendices
PONT. REMY	1916 Jan 28		Refilling point for 139 Bde established at Longpre. The 1st Bde R.F.A., 1st Fld Amb, front of 10th Bde R.F.A. and Sanitary Section arrived.	R.I.
	29th		2nd & 4th Bdes R.F.A., Divl. Train, 3rd Field Amb, ½ R.E. M., 2nd Fld Amb, ½/1 Field C. Rt., R.E. details, 138 Bde Hqrs at Leicester, and part of 3rd Lincolns detrained Tuesday.	R.I. / R.T.
	30th		3rd Line, details 137 Inf Bde, and various other details detrained.	R.I.
	31st		½/1 and 1/2 transport details, not animals arrived by road from rear attached Refilling point for 138th Bde established at Airby to this Clauses. The supply echelon of 138th Division the arrived on 22nd inst attached to our supply echelon for instruction.	R.I.

R Robinson Capt
acting Major
Senior Supply Officer,
40th Division.

Confidential

46 Div Supply Co
Vol #x

War Diary
of
Senior Supply Officer
46ᵗʰ Division
EGYPT
January 1ˢᵗ to February 9ᵗʰ
1916

Wade
Major,
Senior Supply Officer,
46th Division.

WAR DIARY
or
INTELLIGENCE SUMMARY.
(Erase heading not required.)

Army Form C. 2118.

Place	Date	Hour	Summary of Events and Information	Remarks and references to Appendices
MARSEILLES	Jan 1		Arrangements for supplies and embarking supplies &c. Embarked on HMS MAGNIFICENT with Infantry of 137 Bde.	
	2			
	3		Voyage	
	4			
	5			
	6			
	7			
M.E.F. EGYPT	8		Arrival at ALEXANDRIA Harbour.	
	9		Disembarked and arrangements made of Entrainment to tents entrainment. Entrained 2.15 p.m.	
	10		Arrived at KUBRI junction 6 o'clock a.m. Tents arrived &c left of the previous evening. Commenced to such as we had known long and arrange for steady supply of these and tents.	
	11		Arrangements for further supplies to supply to be sent at once and ...	

WAR DIARY
or
INTELLIGENCE SUMMARY
(Erase heading not required.)

Army Form C. 2118.

Place	Date	Hour	Summary of Events and Information	Remarks and references to Appendices
SHALLUFA EGYPT	Jan 12		Formation of Supply Depots in each of Sub-areas. Orders for supplementary bread supply Depot to areas issued by Senior Supply Officer when Groups & Temporary supply Depots outflows O.C. my Depot M/T Supply that up to the purpose of every issue to Unit through Supply Depot to 157 Brigade, and keeping of three such Depots Second Supply in the Checked Issues which amongst to a Fuel Bowl conveyed to our Canal and distributed in particular to Mick & Lejeu. Two groups 9 units to serve the Age by such transport to Quarry One Two.	
	.13.		Issued of Camel Corps for Rations and One emergency of	
	.14.		Units Headquarters of Desert Corps of four surrounding Taurion, Camel Corps, Mule Corps Itubo out in to Sarapin, Generation of Air Ambulance Station.	
	.15.		In tooto Generation of a Air Ambulance of Shalluf, supplies deliveries of Ait Brikat section.	

WAR DIARY or INTELLIGENCE SUMMARY

Army Form C. 2118.

Place	Date	Hour	Summary of Events and Information	Remarks and references to Appendices
SHALLUFA EGYPT	Jan 6		The advanced instructions received from D. of S. I. W. E. F. commenced to form supply Dept on eastern bank to maintain 9 complete days rations for 20,000 men and 9 days' for 5,000 horses. Obliging supplies from front were not enough. Dept duly ???? by light which came up the canal daily. Rlelieved also relieved empty the afternoon. Obtained working parties of 200 to 400 daily from the Infantry to unload supplies on D.B.C.; blanket supplies were supplied to Dept. A. Brigade tents were in charge. Breakable utensils were to be taken back daily from the eastern bank Dept to render the experience of troops. Dept. Supply Officer, 138° Brigade. Army M. ?	

Stores { British 5000
        { Indian 25
        { Egyptian 228

Animals (Camels) (Egypt) 395
                 (Mules) (Indian) 42
                 Horses 2

Army Form C. 2118.

WAR DIARY
or
INTELLIGENCE SUMMARY.
(Erase heading not required.)

Instructions regarding War Diaries and Intelligence Summaries are contained in F.S. Regs., Part II. and the Staff Manual respectively. Title pages will be prepared in manuscript.

Place	Date	Hour	Summary of Events and Information	Remarks and references to Appendices
SHALUFA, EGYPT	July 18		General supervision and verification of formation of Brootion Bank Supply Depot.	
	19		Ditto	
	20		Obtained all Camel Retivro and Indian and Egyptian requirements from Suez back and formed a depot for Trap; together with M.S. wrong by Rifle were verified, sorted and earthy, contributed, so it was then employed to camp horses and carry ato to the railway, back going to the rails supply by horse from the Canal rails, several men ordered and arrangements	
	21		Ditto	
	22		Ditto	
	23		General supervision and arrangements. Correspondence, Returns, Supplies, Issues, of general supervision	

1577 Wt. W10791/1773 500,000 1/15 D. D. & L. A.D.S.S./Forms/C. 2118.

WAR DIARY
or
INTELLIGENCE SUMMARY

Army Form C. 2118.

Place	Date	Hour	Summary of Events and Information	Remarks and references to Appendices
SHALLUFA EGYPT.	Jan 24th		General supervision – Went from Shallufa to Suez Junction and thence went for the purpose of inspecting the 36th Field Bakery at Suez Camp under instructions received from O i/c A.S.C. inspecting the ways to employ such troops received from the A.S.M.I. inspecting the receipt of the Bread. Found the Bakery working well and without serious internal or external difficulties. My two men at work in fuel wood, and no means of storing it. Bins so few as to show the ovens exist but to be stacked on tarpaulins on the ground. Brought samples of the departmental and also rendered supply representing lots deliver. Fuel Wood and two stoves which are very little like to last very long. Refer to reserve supply the bread. Visited Senior Supply Officer, Suez Docks, and arranged with supply officer to despatch of supplies and consignments of supplies and other material to the unit.	

Jones Lieutenant

Army Form C. 2118.

WAR DIARY
or
INTELLIGENCE SUMMARY.
(Erase heading not required.)

Place	Date	Hour	Summary of Events and Information	Remarks and references to Appendices
SHALLUFA EGYPT.	Jan 1		General supervision. Stock in Depot this day after issues:- Biscuit 111,900 - Preserved meat 136,100 - Groceries 6000 - Fuel wood 120 tons - coal 15 tons. Bacon 100,800 lbs. Cheese 128,000 lbs. Dhurra 110,000 lbs. Potatoes 30,676 lbs. Sun Rations 30,000 - Camel Rations complete 2570 - Egyptian Rations complete 1368 - Sudan Rations complete 150. General Supervision of all N.C.O. Details and Supply Depot.	
	28			
	29		Ditto.	
	30		Handed over Depot to O.C.D.C.S. and "Supply Officer 42nd Division". Reports completed with quantities of supplies & R.T. S.A.A. &c &c.	
SIDI BISHR CAMP ALEXANDRIA	31		Left Shallufa by train at 7:0pm with two Brigade Supply Officers, other Depot Details, and my Kit. Arrived Alexandria. Arranged for trucks to be moved by myself and supplies drawn from Emergency Depôt.	

D. W. Coleman, Major,
Senior Supply Officer.

Army Form C. 2118.

WAR DIARY
or
INTELLIGENCE SUMMARY.
(Erase heading not required.)

Instructions regarding War Diaries and Intelligence Summaries are contained in F. S. Regs., Part II. and the Staff Manual respectively. Title pages will be prepared in manuscript.

Place	Date	Hour	Summary of Events and Information	Remarks and references to Appendices
SIDI BISHR	1		General Supervision	
	2		Ditto	
	3		Ditto	
ALEXANDRIA	4		Embarked 4.0 pm on H.M.S. H.T. "MEGANTIC"	
	5		Sailed from ALEXANDRIA at noon	
	6		Voyage – Daily parade A.S. details	
	7		Ditto	
	8		Ditto	
	9		Arrived MARSEILLES – 11.0 a.m. Arranged in clubs to clean up and to welcome reliefs from Base Supply Depot and to interview officers and buy up supply officers. Left South Sheds, Marseille 7.0 p.m. Arrived Pont de Cher Station Quay 10.45 a.m. 1.15 p.m. and issued dinner 5.30 p.m.	

1577 Wt.W10791/1773 500,000 1/15 D. D. & L. A.D.S.S./Forms/C. 2118.

Confidential

46 Div Supply / Feb / Vol IX

War Diary
of
Senior Supply Officer
46th Division
Volume III
February 1st to 29th 1916

[signature]
Major,
Senior Supply Officer,
46th Division.

WAR DIARY
or
INTELLIGENCE SUMMARY.

Army Form C. 2118.

(Erase heading not required.)

Place	Date	Hour	Summary of Events and Information	Strength		Remarks and references to Appendices
				Men	Animals	
PONT RÉMY	1916 Aug 1st		General supervision of Supply arrangements.	10,500	4785	R.J.
"	" 2nd		do. do. do.	10,817	4907	R.J.
"	" 3rd		do. do. do.	10,932	4923	R.J.
"	" 4th		10.20 hrs. First through draught arrived. 1st W draught remain at 6 blo. the following details of the 33 Div. Hellen taken over from 36th Division:- C.R.A., part 1st Metcd. and Cheshire Ammo. R.P.A. 4th Heavy Bde R.F.A., 113th Aux. Whals. All refitted at own 139th Inf. Bde. dump.	12,216	6459	
"	" 5th		57th Div. Arty. Hqrs. part 1st Metcd. and Cheshire Ammo. R.F.A. entrain. today.	11,678	5692	R.J.
"	" 6th		4th Heavy Bde R.F.A. entrains today. A.S.C. details remain and are attached to 46th Div. train. Arrangements made for an issue of flour in lieu of bread or biscuits to 139 Bde.	11,017	5720	R.J.
"	" 7th		General supervision of Supply arrangements.	11,016	4959	R.J.
"	" 8th		do. do.	10,840	5024	R.J.
"	" 9th		2/L Bull to Candas. Special action of Supply	10,877	3032	R.J.

WAR DIARY
or
INTELLIGENCE SUMMARY.

Army Form C. 2118.

(Erase heading not required.)

Place	Date	Hour	Summary of Events and Information	Remarks and references to Appendices
PONT. REMY.	1916 Feb 9th (contd)		Column sent to Candas church with supplies. Wire received from 1st Army instructing us to take on the following units from the 19th Division for issue on 13th inst.:- 36th Divl. Ammn Col, 19th Bde Ammn Col, 1st Cambridge Bn., and 1st Army School. Visited R.U.S.D. 3rd Army and made various arrangements, including a double loading of supply column on 13th inst. at railhead. Major Pickle ASC 11th Division returned at 7.0pm from Egypt. Supply arrangements handed over.	R.S.

R. Tomlinson Capt
acting Senior Supply Officer
46th Division

Army Form C. 2118.

WAR DIARY
or
INTELLIGENCE SUMMARY.
(Erase heading not required.)

Instructions regarding War Diaries and Intelligence Summaries are contained in F. S. Regs., Part II. and the Staff Manual respectively. Title pages will be prepared in manuscript.

Place	Date	Hour	Summary of Events and Information	Strength		Remarks and references to Appendices
PONT REMY	Feb 10		General supervision. Routine supplies and R.P.	10840	5024	—
	11		Ditto	10899	5079	—
	12		Ditto	15087	6235	—
	13		Change of Refilling Point and evacuation of wounded	14076	4654	—
	14		General Supervision	15501	4812	—
	15		Ditto	18686	4726	—
	16		Change of Railway from Longpré to Condien.	14468	4951	—
	17		Routine - Refilling Points. Rail arrangements & Office	14740	5581	—
	18		Ditto	15492	4410	—
	19		D.R.	15797	4778	—
	20		General Supervision. R.O. absent sick	15545	4791	—
	21		Move Ford M.T. from Pont Remy to Domesmont.	14839	4871	—
DOMESMONT	22		General supervision, arranging from P.P. and R.P.	11896	4454	—
	23		Routine, Refilling Point. Rail arrangements, supervision	14616	4072	—
	24		Local Supplies. Office, &c.	15551	4161	—
	25		Ditto	14067	4148	—

1577 Wt. W10791/1773 500,000 1/15 D. D. & L. A.D.S.S./Forms/C. 2118.

Army Form C. 2118.

WAR DIARY
or
INTELLIGENCE SUMMARY.
(Erase heading not required.)

Place	Date	Hour	Summary of Events and Information	Men	Horses	Remarks and references to Appendices
DOMESMARTIN	Feb. 26		Railhead. Refitting Park. Usual arrangements to Independence	14063	4254	
"	27		Local Purchase and General Supervision.	13150	4030	
"	28		Re-arrival of Pumps and Refitting Park in area of Divas.	13165	4165	
DOULLENS	29		Divn H.Q. moved to Doullens. Refitting Park for March 1st:- 137 Bde. HARDINVAL – 138 Bde. BEAUVAL – 139 Bde. DOULLENS. Divl Tps. AUTHEUX. Arrangements for forming new dumps and for fuel supplies also for times for filling in the arrival of troops in new area. Issue of circular of instructions to Supply and Respective Officers. On 27" and 28" supplies were drawn from Railhead by the transport which loaded up for the whole Division in pair on 2 trains – delivered to R.gs. for supplies to be destroyed and then took them onto GE. Mark. Arrival of New Divisional Supply Officers.	15078	4330	

J.S.G. Major
Senior Supply Officer
4th Division

Confidential

War Diary
of
Senior Supply Officer
46th Division
Volume XII
From March 1st to 31st
1916.

Army Form C. 2118.

WAR DIARY
or
INTELLIGENCE SUMMARY.

(Erase heading not required.)

Instructions regarding War Diaries and Intelligence Summaries are contained in F.S. Regs., Part II. and the Staff Manual respectively. Title pages will be prepared in manuscript.

Place	Date	Hour	Summary of Events and Information	Officers	Strength Other Ranks	H.D.	L.D.	Mules	Remarks and references to Appendices
DOULLENS	Mch 1		General supervision of supply arrangements during month		14875	270	3050 269	996	A.
"	" 2		Ditto	14868	295	221	352	996	"
"	" 3		Horse and mules, Railhead and Refilling Point &c. Ditto	14712	295	229	352	959	"
"	" 4		Ditto	14598	310	173	300	867	"
"	" 5		Arrangements for supplies during manoeuvres Ditto	15191	316	257	321	870	"
LE CAUROY	" 6		Ditto	15516	316	632	3618	915	"
"	" 7		Change of Railhead from Candas to Doullens arranged	15869	354	357	3927	963	"
"	" 8		General Supervision and arrangements for supplies during movements of troops	16051	343	189	3957	960	"
"	" 9		and also of Divisions taking over	16279	236	299	2953	1030	"
"	" 10		and also from the 12me Corps Francais	17180	236	300	2962	1027	"
CANDAS	" 11			18576	236	497	4031	1031	"
LIGNY	" 12		arrangements with the Sous-Intendant of the French Army for Today and Tomorrow	17441	372	240	392	1027	"
"	" 13		of Bran Coke Charcoal Fuel Wood	17231	584	265	389	1022	"
"	" 14		and Potatoes Rations were very scarce	17745	356	238	4031	1022	"
"	" 15		to A.D.S. & T. IV Army	18007	293	469	3814	989	"
"	" 16			18777	294	281	3944	1021	"

1577 Wt. W10791/1773 500,000 1/15 D. D. & L. A.D.S.S./Forms/C. 2118.

Army Form C. 2118.

WAR DIARY
or
INTELLIGENCE SUMMARY.
(Erase heading not required.)

Place	Date	Hour	Summary of Events and Information	Strength				Remarks and references to Appendices
				Officers Other ranks	Sick MD	RD	Males	
AMBULANCE L'MBG	Nov 17		General supervision of supply all equipment	19993	262	267	289	1065	Ds
	18		Correspondence. Received. Sent nightly.	19116	259	270	850	781	Ds
	19		Retiring Points.	19209	259	305	4633	987	Ds
	20		Ditto	19588	265	247	4351	992	Ds
	21		Ditto	19545	217	443	4037	1054	Ds
	22		Ditto	18680	295	368	3898	1058	Ds
	23		Ditto	18963	310	250	4124	1051	Ds
	24		General supervision and arrangements for	19169	421	1111	4117	1013	Ds
	25		Mess supply, boots, clothes etc to hinder.	19138	304	340	4309	989	Ds
	26		Cont. for cooking and baking etc for	19705	310	259	4520	990	Ds
	27		Arrangements for details to hospitals	19800	310	222	4185	965	Ds
	28		Arrangements for details to hospitals.	20009	311	259	4121	1011	Ds
	29		Asked Col. R.R. Heard, Reserves and sup.	20579	305	258	4228	1067	Ds
	30		Sent. Church Parties On and Sup.	19701	325	216	4130	1024	Ds
	31		Sect in supervision for Divisional HQ.	19555	324	245	4241	1028	Ds

CONFIDENTIAL.

WAR DIARY

OF

SENIOR SUPPLY OFFICER

46TH. DIVISION

VOLUME ~~X~~ V

From April 1st. to April 30th. 1916

Army Form C. 2118.

WAR DIARY
or
INTELLIGENCE SUMMARY.
(Erase heading not required.)

Instructions regarding War Diaries and Intelligence Summaries are contained in F. S. Regs., Part II and the Staff Manual respectively. Title pages will be prepared in manuscript.

Place	Date	Hour	Summary of Events and Information	STRENGTH				Remarks and references to Appendices
				Officers / Men / Horses	N.D.	L.D.	Mules	
CAMBLAIN L'ABBE	Apl 1		General supervision of supply arrangements	22741 352	214	399	1089	D.S.
	" 2		Ditto	20932 351	191	413	1089	D.S.
	" 3		Ditto	20046 351	190	407	1026	D.S.
	" 4		Ditto	20635 385	205	418	1056	D.S.
	" 5		Ditto	20606 351	196	403	1017	D.S.
	" 6		Ditto	20577 351	205	407	1020	D.S.
	" 7		Ditto	20515 352	196	407	1088	D.S.
	" 8		Ditto	20445 352	196	418	1023	D.S.
	" 9		Ditto	22607 352	189	425	1036	D.S.
	" 10		Ditto	22220 369	191	463	1057	D.S.
	" 11		Ditto	21316 369	191	420	1040	D.S.
	" 12		Correspondence visiting Dist. N.2. Railhead	20986 340	207	423	1056	D.S.
	" 13		Refilling points	20880 340	207	414	1112	D.S.
	" 14		Gen. Arrangements and Distribution	20932 340	212	434	1120	D.S.
	" 15		Refiel Points, entering and arrangements	20964 335	219	449	1127	D.S.
	" 16		for local purchase	21084 337	219	453	1127	D.S.

WAR DIARY or INTELLIGENCE SUMMARY

Army Form C. 2118.

(Erase heading not required.)

Place	Date	Hour	Summary of Events and Information	Officers		Other Ranks			Remarks and references to Appendices
				Sick	Casuals	Sick	WD	LD Cas.	
CAMBLAIN L'ABBE	Apl.17		General acceptance of Supply arrangements	21130	335	219	1117	1117	
	18		Rations - Refuges - Refilling Points - Div	21706	337	215	1102	1081	
	19		Depots - Cambligné	20968	337	231	1125	1062	
	20		Art Row - 138ᵗʰ Bgde as others visited	23198	331	241	1058	1035	
	21		Cambligné. 139ᵗʰ Bgde. Area	20974	284	241	1044	1036	
	22		Arrangements for supplies in new Divisional area	15007	253	156	5309	750	
TINCQUES	23		Rations. St. Pol. Refilling Points. Div. Deplts	14585	214	219	5757	784	
	24		St Michel. 137ᵗʰ Brigade and 138ᵗʰ Brigade St. Pol.	14744	366	213	3818	3818	
	25		Aubigny Road, sent Buicul on Boiritello	14746	368	176	3705	778	
	26		139ᵗʰ Bgade. Diner Section of R.A.S.C.	14726	304	175	3696	819	
	27		left in old area refitted as Embryoned	14586	302	165	3744	810	
	28		General experience of supply arrangements	13865	319	175	3788	831	
	29		D.A.C.	13276	288	139	3747	855	
	30		D.C.	13125	296	112	3094	780	

A. Dawson
A.D.C. 46ᵗʰ Division

Confidential

War Diary

of

Senior Supply Officer

46th Division

From May 1st to 31st 1916

Volume ~~III~~

Army Form C. 2118.

WAR DIARY
or
INTELLIGENCE SUMMARY.
(Erase heading not required.)

Instructions regarding War Diaries and Intelligence Summaries are contained in F. S. Regs., Part II. and the Staff Manual respectively. Title pages will be prepared in manuscript.

Hour, Date, Place	Summary of Events and Information	Remarks and references to Appendices	STRENGTH				
			Officers	Men	Horses	H.D.	L.D. Mules
TINQUES — May 1	General supervision of supply arrangements to attacking Ratters. Refilling points — Saul and Ly Table arrangements Ker Buchan — Collaboration stationary Divisional Forward Section with O.C. Div. Train		13179		310	114	3451 773
" 2	Ditto		14185		319	116	3591 874
" 3	Ditto		15096		191	239	3944 827
" 4	Ditto — supply new area		13504		189	229	3980 822
" 5	Ditto — arrangements for reducing		14316		264	187	3969 683
" 6	Ditto		14056		243	131	3531 896
" 7	Arrangement to supply to Refilling points in the new area. Handing over stores and in new area — Handing over stores and taking over Saul and Review relations in refilling points		13620		156	344	3460 896
" 8	Drew MO stores from Divisional to Clulier St Ouman and Henderens.		16660		318	190	3715 1003
SOLFERINO " 9	General supervision		17599		147	160	3693 1019

Army Form C. 2118.

WAR DIARY
or
INTELLIGENCE SUMMARY.
(Erase heading not required.)

Instructions regarding War Diaries and Intelligence Summaries are contained in F.S. Regs., Part II. and the Staff Manual respectively. Title pages will be prepared in manuscript.

Hour, Date, Place	Summary of Events and Information	STRENGTH					Remarks and references to Appendices
		Officers	Shires	MD	LB	Mules	
SOLERINO Mar 10	General Information	17205	300	567	3971	1051	
11	Ditto	19158	200/1238	3918	1092		
12	Correspondence Div HQ. Reflect bomb go-	16607	273	291	3806	1130	
13	General Information and Raiders	17289	271	292	3780	1088	
14	Ditto	19451	761	292	3925	1077	
15	Investigate to find out for H front and	18510	752	245	3675	1077	
16	General information of Supply arrangements	16234	755	247	3977	1077	
17	Ditto	19246	737	241	3755	1072	
18	Ditto	18891	740	257	3977	1072	
19	Ditto	18697	734	255	3790	1092	
20	Correspondence Div HQ. Reflect bomb Raiders	18387	734	253	3952	1070	
	everyday to seems control Doubture						
	with SC mm						
21	Ditto	18170	736	339	3910	1066	
22	Ditto	18923	778	351	3762	1065	
23	Ditto	19246	831	278	3819	1179	
24	Ditto	19133	831	278	3720	1079	
25	Order preparing Div HQ. Starting forward and	18689	795	276	3567	1033	
	urgently being limited carefully left						
	for latins packing in ever the with						
	troops of Main Column						

Army Form C. 2118.

WAR DIARY
or
INTELLIGENCE SUMMARY.

(Erase heading not required.)

Instructions regarding War Diaries and Intelligence Summaries are contained in F. S. Regs., Part II. and the Staff Manual respectively. Title pages will be prepared in manuscript.

Hour, Date, Place	Summary of Events and Information		STRENGTH		Remarks and references to Appendices
		Officers	Other Ranks / L.D. Men	Animals	
SOLERNAU Mar 26	Second internment of supply arrangements		19137	812	2415 380 9/097 See
" 27	Ditto		19074	808	2413 377 1061 See
" 28	Ditto		19251	812	2413 395 1062 See
" 29	Ditto		19214	815	Dues 371 1060 See
" 30	Ditto		18891	811	2412 356 1080 See
" 31	Ditto		18854	647	2413 049 1080 See

[signature]

(B 20 6) W 3332—1107 100,000 10/13 H W V Forms/C. 2118/10.

Confidential

TRAIN No 15

Division 46

War Diary
of
Senior Supply Officer
46th Division

From June 1st To 30th.

Volume 15

Confidential

WAR DIARY or INTELLIGENCE SUMMARY

Army Form C. 2118.

Place	Hour, Date	Summary of Events and Information	Ranks	Shires	HD	LD	Mules	Remarks
SOLESMES - PAS - WARINCOURT	June 1	Rentrad Bouguenevers & Retiring points	18427	427	249	3670	1083	
	2	Ditto - General supervision	18562	426	241	3653	1105	
	3	Ditto	18553	428	248	3656	1091	
	June 4	Retiring points - Rentrad and Chain companies	18334	448	248	3653	1089	
	5	Advanced area - FONQUEVILLERS - to Reconstation Dumps	18801	430	242	3644	1091	
	6	General supervision	18573	529	138	3647	1089	
	7	Ditto	19094	536	142	3645	1089	
	8	Ditto	19152	549	144	3653	1106	
	9	Advanced area re arrangement to be Reconstation	18832	565	142	3636	1106	
	10	General supervision	18999	562	144	3625	1107	
	11	Ditto	18850	560	135	3771	1100	
	12	Ditto	18865	520	140	3669	1127	
	13	Advanced area re arrangements for Brigade and Divisional Ration Dumps to applicant C.R.E of Divisions and O.C. R.E. Kent.	18705	541	135	5638	1130	
	14	General supervision						
	15	Ditto	19514	529	146	3788	1189	
	16	Retiring points reached and A.S.A. Companies	19094	606	149	3805	1193	
	17	Ditto	19481	604	158	3636	1181	
	18	Ditto	19726	608	158	3644	1174	
			21054	430	249	3653	1210	

Army Form C. 2118.

WAR DIARY
or
INTELLIGENCE SUMMARY.
(Erase heading not required.)

Instructions regarding War Diaries and Intelligence Summaries are contained in F.S. Regs., Part II. and the Staff Manual respectively. Title pages will be prepared in manuscript.

Place	Hour, Date	Summary of Events and Information	Remarks and references to Appendices
SOLERNAU-PAS-WARLINCOURT			**STRENGTH** Officers / Animals / Horses / WD / LD / Mules
	20	January Supervision of supply arrangements	19704 591 150 37 55 1199
	21	Ditto	20100 57 D 142 38 11 1234
	22	Retiring points, D.H.Q. Rations and Corn	19963 572 144 3790 1265
		Companies Ditto	19960 5 1 14 077 1244
	23	Ditto	19803 592 144 3908 1166
	24	Ditto	
	25	Arrangements for fuel, also for troops in hospitals	19972 592 148 2890 1242
	26	Local purchases and Medical comforts	19906 595 170 3889 1273
		Ditto	19582 604 151 3848 1204
	27	Ditto	19742 605 147 3840 1299
	28	Retiring points D.H.Q. Rations and Corn	19637 449 3897 1231
		Companies Ditto	19620 465 148 3894 1221
	29	Ditto	19996 529 145 3897 1219
	30	Ditto	

O.C. coy
L.O.C. lines

Confidential
War Diary
of
Senior Supply Officer
46th Division
from July 1/16 to July 31/1916
Volume XVI

Army Form C. 2118.

WAR DIARY
or
INTELLIGENCE SUMMARY.
(Erase heading not required.)

Instructions regarding War Diaries and Intelligence Summaries are contained in F. S. Regs., Part II. and the Staff Manual respectively. Title pages will be prepared in manuscript.

Place	Date	Hour	Summary of Events and Information	All Ranks	Sh.	H.D.	L.D.	Mules	Remarks and references to Appendices
SOLEMNU	July 1		General revision of supply arrangements	19606	628	144	3794	1172	s/s
PAS	2		Railroad refilling point and train companies	18586	525	142	3772	1117	s/s
WARLINCOURT	3		Ditto (Add 5 for casualties)	14015	404	141	3769	1128	s/s
EWINCOURT	4		Ditto	17651	706	403	3820	1106	s/s
	5								
	6		Local Field ree arrangements &c	17771	751	309	3754	1257	s/s
	6		Div. H.Q. Railhead refilling point &c	18611	707	1130	3656	1250	s/s
	7		Ditto	19325	694	691	3760	1212	s/s
	8		Rendering to D.H.Q. weekly duty Returns						
	8		Divisional Railroad refilling point and Trainbop	19017	684	352	3547	1212	s/s
	9		Ditto	19361	796	286	3851	1212	s/s
	10		Ditto	19506	748	286	3550	1212	s/s
	11		Ditto	18801	492	119	3890	1244	s/s
	12		Ditto	18969	729	258	3784	1213	s/s
	13		Ditto	18942	720	252	3911	1213	s/s
	14		General supervision and arrangement of labour	18935	714	206	3745	1212	s/s
	15		and return from By Divisions	19094	689	259	3608	1216	s/s

1577 Wt.W10791/1773 500,000 1/15 D. D. & L. A.D.S.S./Forms/C. 2118.

WAR DIARY or INTELLIGENCE SUMMARY

Army Form C. 2118.

Place	Date	Hour	Summary of Events and Information	All Ranks	BK	HD	LD	Mules	Remarks
BAVINCOURT	July 16		General Supervision of Supply arrangements	19060	696	259	3619	1215	
	17		O.H.Q. Railhead. Refilling points and Dumbops	19059	677	263	3607	1216	
	18		Ditto	19268	656	263	3650	1221	
	19		Ditto	19250	711	243	3659	1222	
	20		Refilling dumps in Refilling Point. Fuel and	19310	711	243	3644	1218	
	21		distribution and local purchases	19496	711	245	3649	1217	
	22		General Supervision and monthly	19916	701	245	3660	1210	
	23		O.C. Train	20726	697	245	3656	1254	
	24		O.H.Q. Railhead, Refilling points and Train up	20065	698	245	3675	1235	
	25		Ditto	19926	700	223	3681	1235	
	26		Ditto	20537	702	232	3641	1232	
	27		Ditto	20582	711	257	3641	1235	
	28		Arrangements for vegetables, fuel and	21196	691	251	3669	1231	
	29		Local purchase from dy tables, from	21492	686	229	3644	1232	
	30		Supply and welfare requirements	21675	697	229	3691	1235	
	31		General supervision	21210	699	229	3682	1239	

D. Derry
Senior Supply Officer
60th Division

Vol 9

Confidential

War Diary
of
Senior Supply Officer 46th Division

from Aug 1/1916 to Aug 31/1916

Volume XVII

Army Form C. 2118.

WAR DIARY
or
INTELLIGENCE SUMMARY.

(Erase heading not required.)

Instructions regarding War Diaries and Intelligence Summaries are contained in F. S. Regs., Part II. and the Staff Manual respectively. Title pages will be prepared in manuscript.

Place	Date	Hour	Summary of Events and Information	STRENGTH				Remarks and references to Appendices
				Other Ranks	Animals			
					Riding H.D.	H.D.	Mules	
BAVINCOURT	Aug 1		General information	21147	687	329	3695	1235
	2		Railways. Refilling bomb, Steam bomb area.	21491	719	215	3716	1234
	3		Ditto	21086	668	215	3714	1231
	4		Ditto	21137	663	215	3641	1227
	5		Ditto	20651	509	245	3691	1232
	6		Ditto and arrangements for looking after Field and supply of trucks	20905	649	247	3697	1201
	7			21209	740	347	3700	1230
	8			20941	638	247	3695	1230
	9		Ditto	21541	628	347	4422	1233
	10		Interview of safety arrangements	22562	628	260	4577	1240
	11		Ditto	22009	628	353	4599	1229
	12		Ditto	21921	628	251	4579	1236
	13		Ditto	21996	607	251	4626	1198
	14		Ditto	21815	624	251	4587	1304
	15		Ditto	21694	624	251	4560	1305
	16		Ditto	21679	624	250	4654	1298

WAR DIARY or INTELLIGENCE SUMMARY

Army Form C. 2118.

Place	Date	Hour	Summary of Events and Information	Remarks and references to Appendices
BAVINCOURT	Aug 17		General supervision of supply arrangements	
	18		Railhead D.H.Q. Refilling points & chain horse	
	19		Ditto	
	20		Ditto	
	21		Ditto	
	22		Ditto	
	23		Ditto	
	24		Ditto	
	25		Moved with Division from Bavincourt to BAILLEULMONT	
	26		General Supervision R.H. & Divisional Supplies at BAILLEULMONT	
	27		Railhead Refilling points & Chain horse	
	28		General supervision of Supply arrangements	
	29		Ditto	
	30		Ditto	
	31		Ditto	

STRENGTH

	All Ranks	Horses	M.D.	L.D.	Mules
	21304	627	250	4599	1297
	21824	621	250	4700	1298
	21519	621	251	4741	1297
	21942	636	255	4702	1297
	22022	635	255	4706	1300
	21970	627	255	4500	1293
	22022	626	255	5204	1293
	22004	622	255	5706	11111
	22161	621	255	5581	11111
	22185	625	254	5995	11114
	22109	627	254	5882	11114
	21991	634	251	5946	11141
	21954	639	251	5999	1150
	21981	639	251	5857	1157
	21982	678	263	5786	1149

Confidential
War Diary
of
Senior Supply Officer
46th Division

Sept 1st to Sept 30. 1916

(Volume 18.)

WAR DIARY or INTELLIGENCE SUMMARY

Army Form C. 2118.

Place	Date	Hour	Summary of Events and Information	Strength — All Ranks	Shires	Animals HD	LD	Mules	Remarks and references to Appendices
BAINICOURT	1		General return of Supply Column	21659	629	255	5859	1459	
	2		do	21672	629	255	5912	1462	
	3		do	21592	629	255	5876	1481	
	4		do	20804	630	255	3896	1451	
	5		do	20594	629	255	3795	1458	
	6		do	20230	632	255	3699	1459	
	7		do	20562	629	254	3657	1232	
	8		do	19988	629	258	3672	1220	
	9		do	19782	609	258	3702	1220	
	10		do	19861	609	258	3696	1222	
	11		do	20232	607	258	4196	1231	
	12		do	19797	600	259	3627	1222	
	13		do	19852	590	259	3592	1231	
	14		do	20051	586	259	3592	1218	
	15		Do. Handed over to Capt. (illegible)	19963	730	259	3532	1916	
	16		do	20558		259		1214	

Army Form C. 2118.

WAR DIARY
or
INTELLIGENCE SUMMARY.
(Erase heading not required.)

Instructions regarding War Diaries and Intelligence Summaries are contained in F. S. Regs., Part II. and the Staff Manual respectively. Title pages will be prepared in manuscript.

Place	Date	Hour	Summary of Events and Information	All Ranks/Shires	STRENGTH Animals HD LD	An/LS	Remarks and references to Appendices
Bannockburn	17		General interviews Rickshaw etc	19136	738	721 3645	1206	90
	18		Cyclist Tour	19372	742	259 3656	1201	90
	19		Arrangements for 2nd manoeuvres etc	18881	744	259 3652	1201	90
	20		Road purchases etc	19149	740	259 3513	1202	90
	21		Ditto	19159	731	259 3506	1206	90
	22							
	23		Cycle Chennai etc	19341	732	259 3502	1202	90
	24		General Supervision	19181	774	220 3508	1212	90
	25		Rifle	18580	772	220 3510	1202	90
	26		Stand over to Major Wilcluff	19083	785	220 3531	1204	90
	27		General Supervision and response to	19117	772	220 3519	1206	90
	28		Sr briefing ready party of 16	18994	767	219 3528	1205	90
	29		Inspection action	19142	775	721 3611	1208	90
	30			19188	786	222 3614	1205	90
	31		General Supervision	19120	771	259 3539	1202	90
			Ditto					

Bredward
Lt. Col. D.V. Evans

Confidential
War Diary
of
Senior Supply Officer 46th Division
from Oct 1/1916 to Oct 31/1916

Volume XIX

46th Div
Senior Suppl Officer

Army Form C. 2118.

WAR DIARY
or
INTELLIGENCE SUMMARY.
(Erase heading not required.)

Instructions regarding War Diaries and Intelligence Summaries are contained in F. S. Regs., Part II. and the Staff Manual respectively. Title pages will be prepared in manuscript.

Place	Date	Hour	Summary of Events and Information	STRENGTH						Remarks and references to Appendices
				Officers Others	Shirts	Animals H.D.	L.D.	Mob-3		
BAYINCOURT	Oct 1		General Supervision of Supply Services	19071	777	225	3555	1208		
"	2		Raillead correspondence D.A.D. Refilling points	19022	777	225	3508	1204		
"	3		11th and 49th Divs. in attachment of Divn R.T.	19056	819	225	3522	1204		
"	4		Issued Rations to mgd. Divn R.A.M.C. Coy 146 MG Batty. DAL	22982	823	508	5922	1849		
"	5		General supervision of supply services	22942	822	508	5925	1848		
"	6		Change Stars of Retail unves of Kitchen	23116	842	501	5921	1818		
"	7		Railhead and Refilling points	22970	848	481	5907	1814		
"	8		Ditto	22820	890	479	5875	1814		
"	9		gug R.F. loss with Supply Wagons direct	22881	901	465	5893	1818		
"	10		Railhead Refilling Points and Seal Purchases	22667	896	465	5859	1813		
"	11		Transported Wood purchases	22862	890	465	5865	1806		
"	12		General supervision	22548	890	465	5871	1806		
"	13		Ditto	22817	889	471	5879	1801		
"	14		Ditto	22930	887	469	5886	1800		
"	15		Ditto	22763	946	407	5886	1796		
"	16		Ditto	22993	947	403	5855	1791		

Army Supply Nuus [?]
46 Div

Army Form C. 2118.

WAR DIARY
or
INTELLIGENCE SUMMARY.
(Erase heading not required.)

Place	Date	Hour	Summary of Events and Information	All Ranks & Shires	Animals HD	LD	Mules	Remarks and references to Appendices
DAINEOURT	Oct 17		General Supervision of Supply arrangements	22917	860	400	5868	1804	
	18		at view to using the Motor RJ at	22976	861	400	5850	1803	
	19		Railhead and Refilling Points	19109	893	156	3577	1193	
	20		Ditto	19023	901	156	3671	1193	
	21		Ditto	18905	894	159	3588	1022	
	22		Ditto	18694	893	159	3562	1196	
	23		General Supervision	18505	894	159	3557	1195	
	24		Ditto	18014	894	158	3558	1194	
	25		Ditto	18775	894	159	3542	1190	
	26		Ditto	18801	894	159	3542	1191	
	27		Ditto	19033	894	159	3543	1194	
	28		Arrangements with the Divisional Train convoys for	19128	890	159	3663	1241	
	29		ration to the RJ Dump and Motor RJ used	19976	899	159	3655	1319	
	30		the Mules also the Refilling Points indeed Supply	13125	194	51	1068	655	
	31		Reserve Rations in Separating Points to	13326	182	55	1050	655	

1577 Wt.W.10791/1773 500,000 1/15 D. D. & L. A.D.S.S/Forms/C. 2118.

Secret.

Confidential

War Diary

of

Senior Supply Officer 46th Division

from Nov 1/1916 to Nov 30/1916

Volume XX

WAR DIARY
or
INTELLIGENCE SUMMARY.

Army Form C. 2118.

(Erase heading not required.)

Senior Supply Officer 46th Div.

Place	Date	Hour	Summary of Events and Information	STRENGTH					Remarks and references to Appendices
				All Ranks	Horses	Animals H.D.	L.D.	Mules	
FROHEN. LE·GRAND									
BAILLEUCOURT	1		No.1 Arrangements for supplies during move of Division	13476	186	59	1205	854	
ST RIQUIER	2		Ditto	13251	170	65	1176	852	
"	3		Reviewing parts In. and Refilling points	13195	154	69	1180	850	
"	4		Ditto	13257	154	97	1185	844	
"	5		General supervision at Railhead and Dumps	13210	216	83	1184	844	
"	6		Conferences and D.N.A. matters and	13433	195	55	1188	842	
"	7		Arrangements with D.P. Os. for Hay and	13449	195	59	1188	840	
"	8		Straw	13392	195	50	1181	844	
"	9		Gnl. arrangements and correspondence	13280	195	60	1183	835	
"	10		General supervision and rectifying Demands	13375	205	51	1198	821	
"	11		transport receipts	14394	199	60	1297	908	
"	12		Ditto	14499	198	61	1294	906	
"	13		Ditto	14468	210	62	1297	908	
"	14		Ditto	14699	201	60	1294	910	
"	15		Ditto	14521	201	61	1225	902	
"	16		Ditto	14614	200	61	1230	900	

WAR DIARY or INTELLIGENCE SUMMARY

Army Form C. 2118.

Junior Supply Hone
46 Div =

Place	Date	Hour	Summary of Events and Information	All Ranks	Strength Ships	Animals UD	LD	Mules	Remarks and references to Appendices
ST KIDVIER	18		General and temporary Supply Arrangements	14588	200	62	1222	898	
"	19		Ditto	14610	200	61	1239	899	
"	20		Ditto	14400	200	61	1240	899	
"	21		Ditto	14348	200	61	1251	901	
"	22		Ditto	14279	200	67	1258	901	
"	23		Arrangements made in event of movement Rydoui	14117	209	67	1226	898	
"	24		Similar preps for contingencies arrangements to	14211	205	76	1221	897	
ROUEN LE GRAND	25		Ditto	14244	189	94	1219	897	
LUCHEUX	26		Arrangements for teams and implements they	14508	195	96	1222	897	
"	27		"	14468	193	106	1210	898	
"	28		General experiences	14301	189	91	1242	896	
"	29		Ditto	14256	291	91	1279	897	
"	30		Ditto	14242	212	82	1225	895	
"	30			14245	400	72	1205	900	

46 Div RA

Confidential

War Diary of
Senior Supply Officer

46th Division

From 1.12.16 to 31.12.16.

(Volume   )

WAR DIARY
or
INTELLIGENCE SUMMARY.

(Erase heading not required.)

Army: Devon Supply Officer, 40th Division

Place	Date	Hour	Summary of Events and Information	All Ranks	Shires	Animals HD.	L.D.	Mules	Remarks and references to Appendices
LUCHEUX	Dec 1		General inspection of Supply arrangements	14455	180	70	1522	897	
"	2		Ditto	14225	189	73	1251	898	
"	3		Ditto	17289	326	72	3584	1180	
"	4		Ditto	17383	306	90	3611	1179	
"	5		Re arrival funds and Reflew funds to new area	14557	171	73	1212	895	
"	6		Arrangements for Indl. Vehicle. Draw L. Vet. Off, AVC grms	15770	189	517	1491	888	
WARLINCOURT	7		Gun 0000 go to hand	16840	507	519	1790	906	
"	8		Rations and Refuller Points	16951	726	376	1752	930	
"	9		Ditto	17772	798	289	1788	927	
"	10		Ditto	17485	629	471	1749	928	
"	11		Ditto	17336	610	475	1769	920	
"	12		Gen Inspection and resorting Rations and AHQ and	17058	865	371	1762	924	
"	13		Refilled Points.	17004	613	466	1770	922	
"	14		Ditto	16945	477	275	1480	923	
"	15		Ditto	16159	1162	315	1489	922	
"	16		Ditto	15795	1444	271	1388	922	

WAR DIARY
or
INTELLIGENCE SUMMARY.
(Erase heading not required.)

I.S.O.
46th Div.

Place	Date	Hour	Summary of Events and Information	All Ranks	Shires	Animals HD	LD	Mules	Remarks and references to Appendices
WARLINCOURT	Diary		General Information of Supply arrangements	16205	443	275	1165	919	
"	18		Ditto	16248	441	275	1469	927	
"	19		Ditto	16139	441	275	1477	923	
"	20		D.S.O. Rations and Refill Points	16022	437	366	1454	900	
"	21		Arrangements for 2nd Words and Distribution of lime	16334	437	291	1500	925	
"	22		" "	16252	439	277	1482	924	
"	23		General Information of Supply arrangements	19322	541	274	3812	1224	
"	24		Ditto	19566	561	275	3798	1204	
"	25		Ditto	19251	577	274	3777	1201	
"	26		Ditto	19990	436	401	3776	1201	
"	27		Ditto	19410	541	274	3778	1201	
"	28		Ditto	19502	542	269	3777	1201	
"	29		Ditto	20000	542	269	3771	1212	
"	30		Ditto	19361	440	276	3770	1212	
"	31		Ditto	19412	512	271	3768	1224	

Confidential

Vol 14

War Diary
of
Senior Supply Officer
46th Divn.

1-1-17 — 31-1-17

(Volume XXIII)

Confidential

WAR DIARY or INTELLIGENCE SUMMARY

Army Form C. 2118.

(Erase heading not required.)

Instructions regarding War Diaries and Intelligence Summaries are contained in F. S. Regs., Part II. and the Staff Manual respectively. Title pages will be prepared in manuscript.

Place	Date	Hour	Summary of Events and Information	STRENGTH					Remarks and references to Appendices
				All Ranks	Horses	Animals M.D.	L.D.	Mules	
WARLINCOURT	Jan 1		General supervision of supply arrangements	19958	439	266	3759	1225	
	2		Ditto	19924	616	80	3755	1242	
	3		Arrangements for forage perfected with R.O. and A.D.	20483	708	—	4226	1288	
	4		Various arrangements with Corps "Q"	20057	706	.	4125	1236	
	5		Arrangements for distribution of boot laces also	20414	706	.	4098	1188	
	6		Both authorised so out, and all arrangements	20229	696		3849	1280	
	7		Conferences D.A.Q.S. Reserve Artillery Park	19977	696		3767	1218	
	8		and various Train Companies with O.C.	20004	689		3904	1290	
	9		General supervision of supply arrangements	20022	690		3954	1279	
	10		Ditto	20473	690		3945	1280	
	11		Ditto	20724	684		3932	1249	
	12		Ditto	20115	684		3917	1243	
	13		Ditto	20120	684		3926	1242	
	14		Ditto	20395	665		11042	1199	
	15		Ditto	20201	680		3900	1253	
	16		Ditto	20070	649		3900	1252	

Army Form C. 2118.

WAR DIARY
or
INTELLIGENCE SUMMARY.
(Erase heading not required.)

Instructions regarding War Diaries and Intelligence Summaries are contained in F. S. Regs., Part II. and the Staff Manual respectively. Title pages will be prepared in manuscript.

Place	Date	Hour	Summary of Events and Information	STRENGTH				Remarks and references to Appendices
				All Ranks	Ranks Shires	Animals H.D	A.D	
WARLINCOURT	Jan 17		General supervision of Supply arrangements	21185	1001		3960	1064
	18		Ditto — Supply Down opened 9.30 am 3.30 pm	21568	1001		3831	1250
	19		Ditto — do — 10.45 am	20948	996		3825	1252
	20		Ditto — do — noon	21341	989		3895	1247
	21		Correspondence and Returns for A.D.S.&T. do — 10.15 am	20709	990		3804	1249
	22		D.H.Q. Ranches Refixing Tanks and issues of Rum	21078	990		3816	1234
	23		Conference with O.C. — Supply Down adding 9.15 am	21105	1159		3787	1252
	24		General supervision of Supply arrangements do — 11.0 am	20999	1081		3762	1238
	25		Ditto — Supply Drawn arrived 6.50pm	20626	1076		3776	1252
	26		Ditto — Supply classes served at noon 27th at 11.45 am	20240	869		3941	1252
	27		Ditto — do — 11 of from 28th	20232	865		3732	1252
	28		Ditto — do — 12.30pm 29, at MONDICOURT	19580	865		3725	1250
	29		Ditto — do — 12 of 29, at WARLINCOURT 6.45 from 30	20280	865		3723	1248
	30		Ditto — do — 2.45 am 6.45 from 31	20168	865		3719	1248
	31		Ditto —	20226	865		3706	1247

1577 Wt.W10791/1773 500,000 1/15 D. D. & L. A.D.S.S./Forms/C. 2118.

Confidential

War Diary
Senior Supply Officer
46th Division

1.2.17 to 28.2.17

Vol. XXIII

WAR DIARY or INTELLIGENCE SUMMARY

Army Form C. 2118.

Senior Supply Officer 46. Div.

Place	Date	Hour	Summary of Events and Information	ALL RANKS	ANIMALS Shires/HD	LD	MT/26	Remarks and references to Appendices
WARLENCOURT	Feb 1		General supervision of supply arrangements	22366	896	3565	1250	
"	2		Arrangements for fuel, wood supply and distribution	20499	852	3904	1273	55th Div Units attached
"	3		Rationing XP'rs and 96th Bde London Inf. of 58th Div	1920	32	94		
"	4		(and other Details attached accordingly. 185 M.T. Coy detached Col.	20368	853	3543	1273	
"	5		from Motor Ambulance Store in Rouen Park 13126 Bde Col.	1920	32	94	1	
"			gave heavy lorry to - D.S. 2nd Lothian Road Control Post	20525	787	3716	1259	
"			H.Q. XVIII Corps H.Q.	1970	26	94	1	
"	6		Arrangements for fresh provisions and extra fuel for line	20698	780	3719	1270	
"			through D.S. Oc.	1910	17	93	1	
"	7			20200	567	3799	1257	
"	8			1000	17	53	1	
"	9			20416	781	3708	1266	
"				1875	17	53	40	
"	10		Ammunition and forage supervision of feeding of animals	22451	927	2798	1233	
"	11		Railhead - M.S.O. Hatry,	22553	858	3826	1240	
"	12			24182	814	2810	1247	
"	13			22325	808	1943	1259	
"	14			22460	802	3753	1245	
"	15			25458	821	3780	1245	
"	16			22799	802	2710	1251	
"				1117	1			
"	17			25087	791	2870	1224	
"					802		1226	

WAR DIARY or INTELLIGENCE SUMMARY

Army Form C. 2118.

Senior Supply Officer
46 Div

Place	Date	Hour	Summary of Events and Information	All Ranks	Sk. y HD	LD	M+ls	Remarks and references to Appendices
WARLINCOURT	Feb 16		General experience of supply arrangements	23542	797	3664	1251	
	17		Ditto	21159 (2368)	416	3824 6	1252	
	18		Ditto	20480	409	3244	1246	
	19		Arrangements for entraining 139 Brigade in trucks area 80.S. 6th Regt also Park Dafer B.T. LE CAUROY	18691	380	3578	1256	
	20		Ditto and general experience	20544	376	3580	1288	
	21		Ditto	21782	381	3600	1294	
	22		Ditto	19784	381	3638	1266	
	23		Ditto	20064	370	3549	1227	
	24		Ditto	20762	368	3564	1234	
	25		Arrangements for carrying out supplementary fuel issue to troops who are shortly to be away on trucks at rate of 10 lbs lower scale	20508	355	3602	1222	
	26			20973	360	3636	1284	
	27			20750	368	3676	1224	
	28		General experience of supply arrangements	20856	362	3593	1206	

Signed
S.S.O. 46th Div

~~Confidential~~ Secret

War Diary

Senior Supply Officer
46th Division

March 1st to 31st 1917.

(Volume) XXIV.

WAR DIARY or INTELLIGENCE SUMMARY

Army Form C. 2118.

Divnl Supply Train
46 Div

Place	Date	Hour	Summary of Events and Information	Ration Strength				Remarks and references to Appendices
				Offrs	S-NCO	O.R.	Mules	
WARLNCOURT	Oct 1st		General extension of supply arrangements.	20239	357	3648	1254	
			Bathing. Refitting finds. Conferences. Fuel + Forage.					
			Medical announces to B.D.S.T. 3316, 3317 for those					
			attached to 250 Rifles etc at the new Divnl Sources					
			Yield. Sounds Inar. Disinfectors, pioneers — police					
			and Orse to Cavarno. Solva DR duties.					
"	2		General afternoon. Routines — Bathing + fitting + others —	20672	359	3673	1244	
			Fuel water and Disinfection. Three Corps Generals.					
			three days arrangements for entraining + detraining					
			supply hundreds etc for Ind Brigade.					
"	3		General afternoon. Routines. Refitting funds & Junr	20548	349	3638	1251	
			Supply Officers.					
"	4		D.M.S	20239	349	3652	1152	
"	5		G.H.C.	20294	347	3653	1229	
"	6		General afternoon. Routines Divnl Units and Try Res	19709	358	3658	1165	
			H.Qrs. DHQ Routines and Refitting Funds.					

WAR DIARY
or
INTELLIGENCE SUMMARY.
(Erase heading not required.)

Army Form C. 2118.

S.S.O. 46 Div.
Minith

Place	Date	Hour	Summary of Events and Information	Cars	Animals		Mules	Remarks and references to Appendices
					S. &D.	r.D		
MARTINCOURT	Mar 7		General supervision of supply arrangements	20160	377	3707	1236	
"	8		D[itt]o					
	9		D[itt]o	20118	367	3680	1934	
	10		Arrangements for Rum and Butter being the issues by units in supply convoy on 11th by supply officer to Batch	20241	367	3670	1934	
	11		General supervision of supply arrangements. Correspondence entry Railway arrangements with R.S.O. S.S.O. on 11th	19975	367	3636	1232	
			to the returning of handbooks. Visited Ratelieu pit. (Blue Supply Officer - D.A.Q.)	19909	365	3690	8021	
	12		Arrangements for railing essentials for use in traffic for	20141	464	3650	1255	
	13		attack ostentibly and means senators to units going	20521	362	3708	1235	
	14		at once transportation - Supply M.V. lorries from	20877	369	3779	1227	
	15		the wounded - and the clearance of the troops contract with units and ...	20279	365	3652	11950	

WAR DIARY or INTELLIGENCE SUMMARY

Army Form C. 2118.

S.S.O. 46 Div.

Place	Date	Hour	Summary of Events and Information	Remarks and references to Appendices
WARLINCOURT	Mar 15th continued		...in a dangerous position now on fire and some 15,000 rounds of ammunition was exposed. The hose arrangements worked by the M.G.S. of necessity the plan for end of the S. fortunate in the [illegible] and supplying water with as much promptly of [illegible] to [illegible] a loss which for months has been [illegible]. Stores. Men helped for ambulances and men after the [illegible] front to G.	
	16		Finished interment of empty ammunition [illegible].	AAC Rnds S-10 HD Rounds
	17		Rations for R.Q. etc loaded, spare [illegible] ammunition.	20516 364 3803 1146
	18		True [illegible] w.	20980 364 3801 1154
	19			20949 358 2786 1106
	20		10 Oct	20246 360 2786 1136
	21		19850 354 2788 1051
			Necessary [illegible] for men in the new ventilated sticks [illegible] arrangement to [illegible] of Stowing the [illegible] stacks of [illegible]. Cut away [illegible] material.	20211 354 2748 991
COUIN	22		Moved to Couin. Arrangements for drawing supplies from new railhead BEAUSSART	20098 319 2753 980

1577 Wt.W10791/1773 500,000 1/15 D.D.&L. A.D.S.S./Forms/C. 2118.

WAR DIARY or INTELLIGENCE SUMMARY

Army Form C. 2118.

S.S.O. 46 Division

STRENGTH

	Ranks	S&WO	ADJ	Murhy
	19703	326	2794	1001

Place	Date	Hour	Summary of Events and Information	Remarks
COUIN	March 23		Routes - BEAUSSART - Visited various and outlying points BERTRANCOURT & BUS. Re-arranging fronts and outlying points for our new - divisional front to extend our front line sectors - Bus Rd and Hebuterne Rd to 2 Coy Infantry - arrangement for shelling and standing men in Rest lines to enable points to be held. g - BIENVILLERS - FONQUEVILLERS - SAILLY-AU-BOIS and GOMMÉCOURT. Touring our attacks that 2 men Plat. GAUDIEMPRÉ - 3/3 cable section 3. 2/2 Lewis Gun Som Platoon SOUASTRE. 1 Infantry details. Emergency Pte. 5 Coy Inf. 5 Cpl. Cyclist. Pte. 1 Batln Inf. 1 Pte. Buonaltena Mots. 45 3/4 sentry points 400 whole Coy and Inmediately outer that covering 2/3 covering covering Infantry 1 member St LEGER 1 ... Mr Bu Rd - Major SAILLY-AU-BOIS - W - Cpl Infantry only 2 Cpl Pueture Bois. T Windmill.		

WAR DIARY or INTELLIGENCE SUMMARY

Army Form C. 2118.

S.S.O. 46 Div.

Place	Date	Hour	Summary of Events and Information	Strength				Remarks and references to Appendices
				Other Ranks	S. & H.Q.	H.Q.	Animal	
	May 1923 continued		Divisional Troops & Sqns to Divks and also attaching a Sapper Officer to each Div Supply Column. Had arrangements to be divisibly preforming now entirely for the Divisions.					
VILLERS BOCAGE	May 24		Routine - BELLE EGLISE. Moved MQ to Villers Bocage. Had arrangement to meet first convey coming to our area. Touring supply Officers and M.S.C.	17333	326	2692	952	✓
	25		Routine - Supply fronts gardo Visit. FRECHENCOURT. BELLE EGLISE. Arrangements for outflow saved further west of Division. Routine - Supply fronts.	14981 2811	555 97	1070 1711	665 470	✓
DURY par Amiens	x		Moved with MQ to DURY. Arrived to Freshest to Extreme party of Light things settled programme and arrived arrangements with Units & extreme would outflow entrust to have on	15061 2802	238 71	1048 1662	671 470	✓

WAR DIARY or INTELLIGENCE SUMMARY

Army Form C. 2118

S.S.O. 46 Division

Place	Date	Hour	Summary of Events and Information	Strength Rank	S&NCO	A.D.	Other	Remarks and references to Appendices
	Month entered		Detained one clerk days rations for (indecipherable) Regt. Issued ammunition and equipment to infantry supplies now on the division. — Supply officer to attain					
			and Rail with the Brigade Train					
DURY	27		Rations — Infantry & Inf — FRECHENCOURT	15031	246	1049	670	
			Artillery Inf. — BELLE EGLISE	2911	69	1845	438	
			Issued supervision and keeping in touch with S.O.					
			Frechencourt and Railhead					
DURY	28		Railhead — Supplying Inf. 138 & 139 bry adv.	8730	181	556	318	
			Artillery Inf. —	6528	148	500	215	
			— do —	2932	86	2040	473	
	29		Railhead — Infantry Hars. Po. VILLERS	15256	254	1050	669	
			Issued supervision of supply ...reinforced	2854	69	946	514	
NORRENT	30		Railhead — Infantry .... VILLERS- Artillery ROSEL	15161 A	250	1050	669	
FONTES				2854 A	96	971	519	
			Issued supervision					
	31		Railhead — Infantry from VILLERS — Artillery FREVENT	16517 A	258	1061	719	
			Issued supervision.	2858 A	73	781	511	

Senior Supply Officer

Confidential

War Diary
of
Senior Supply Officer
46th Division

1.4.17   —   30.4.17

(Vol. XXV)

Army Form C. 2118.

WAR DIARY
or
INTELLIGENCE SUMMARY.
(Erase heading not required.)

Instructions regarding War Diaries and Intelligence Summaries are contained in F. S. Regs., Part II. and the Staff Manual respectively. Title pages will be prepared in manuscript.

Place	Date 1915	Hour	Summary of Events and Information	All Ranks	STRENGTH Animals S & HD	L.D.	Mules	Remarks and references to Appendices
NORRENT FONTES.	Apl. 1st		General supervision of supply services - Rations despatched from LILLERS	15363	253	1060	716	
			Aithay ST POL	2846	73	1761	1462	
	2nd		Ditto Refilling Points - ECQUEDECQUES.	18260	314	2958	1211	
			138 and 139 Brigade AUCHY-AU-BOIS. Div. Troops - NORRENT FONTES.					
			Relieving convoy by road with 451 Coy. A.S.C. and motor 46th Supply Column arrange for Coal 2 tons to be drawn in their own refilling point in reserve for their					
	3		General supervision of supply services. Rations and refilling point 2 Div.	18953	310	2870	1233	
			A & of Batt ENGRS - ST JULIEN returned by special Army Service Supply Column					
			Requirements for Coal supplied by half from Divisional L ST VENANT.					
			The Coal is unloaded by special fatigue party and dumped on site which					
			at end of several days is to Supply depots with 5 wear so many tons.					
			Issues made on chits to the Supply Column Packing Dispos or 1st Corps					
			Dispos or 18th Division.					
	4		General supervision of supply arrangements - Correspondence respecting	18804	293	2790	1266	
			points - Rations. D.H.Q. Headquarters inter Deputy Officers then					
			and generals for supplementing the Army Rations.					

Army Form C. 2118.

WAR DIARY
or
INTELLIGENCE SUMMARY.
(Erase heading not required.)

Instructions regarding War Diaries and Intelligence Summaries are contained in F. S. Regs., Part II. and the Staff Manual respectively. Title pages will be prepared in manuscript.

Place	Date	Hour	Summary of Events and Information	STRENGTH				Remarks and references to Appendices
				All Ranks	Officers S/HD	Animals L.D.	Mules	
NORRENT FONTES	Apl. 5		General supervision of Supply and Transport services. Correspondence. RMA Drew Companies Refilling Points and Railhead.	18239	295	2825	1221	dy/OR
	6		Ditto	18141	301	2754	1220	dy/OR
			Arrangements for a special Issue of 2 Knives of Transport and one Divisional Supply Companies and Issues					
	7		General supervision of Supply and Transport services. Special run in of retired at 5.0pm the G.O.C. proceeds from army	18039	299	2755	1265	dy/OR
	8		Correspondence, Railing RMA, Refilling points and drew Companies. Supervision of Transferring supplies from Supply train at Railhead.	18356	304	2816	1223	dy/OR
	9		General supervision of Supply and Transport arrangements. Detrain loading of supplies from Supply train to Dist. Train as per first orders at Railhead at 2.0pm. Second D.A.D.S.&T. 3rd Corps and others at 3rd Division. Transport organized at various and drew Transport Officers will of Junior Transport Officers monthly - arrangements in connection of troops. No am trying to attempt to clear Michelin town in Domremlin. Supplies taken from various to ordinary dumps at ECQUEDECQUES.	18268	404	2797	1225	dy/OR

1577 Wt. W10791/1773 500,000 1/15 D. D. & L. A.D.S.S./Forms/C. 2118.

Army Form C. 2118.

WAR DIARY
or
INTELLIGENCE SUMMARY.
(Erase heading not required.)

Instructions regarding War Diaries and Intelligence Summaries are contained in F. S. Regs., Part II. and the Staff Manual respectively. Title pages will be prepared in manuscript.

Place	Date	Hour	Summary of Events and Information	Remarks and references to Appendices
NORRENT FONTES	April 9th		There they were entrained from the Echelons of wagons and started and were entrained up and arrived by a supply dump at N.O. 187 Brigade in the evening. Men paraded to own open space and unset ready. — LESPRESSES — When they were informed with porter by a transport Officer special lines for the purpose. By this elements the war unloaded. Wagons with lives to the and dumps at ECQUEDECQUES about 1 the kilometre and wagons supplies out to the respective Refilling points for Troops NORRENT FONTES. 138 & 139 Brigade AUCHY-AU-BOIS. 137 Bde ECQUEDECQUES. The loading at Rail had proceeded very satisfactorily and the whole train - unloaded and any not refilled pour a front locomotive journey from, and the activity of 4 lorries for one truck of hay — none slower in 24 minutes. Loading was carried by the Officers and drivers of supplies at the ordinary dumps than were outposts and the safety arrangements very tactful 60 rounds were ordinary to this respective companies. Orders were issued to the evening respecting transport lorries and supply Columns and	

Sgd. [signature]

WAR DIARY
or
INTELLIGENCE SUMMARY.

(Erase heading not required.)

Army Form C. 2118.

Place	Date	Hour	Summary of Events and Information	STRENGTH				Remarks and references to Appendices
				All Ranks	S&HD	Animals R.D.	Mules	
NORRENT FONTES	April 10		General improvement of supply and transport arrangements. Compliments. Return X. Trials V.A.G. for our Res. units Joined Contractors and Refugees Sections. Afternoon visits to Butchers Killers. Inspection into Meat issues, cups and forfeits in 1 hour 7 min.	18571	3114	S.2734 R.2742	1297	✓
	11		General improvement of supplies and transport arrangements. Res. Out Rations issued for all Army of Horses.	18444	322	S.2727 R.2762	1318	✓
			Dir:					
	12		Met Lt. Genl. Conference LILLERS. BETHUNE Rd. and inspected for horse and war rifle. 451 Coy. BAS RIEUX - Refilling point for Div. Jnyce. L'ECLEME — 452 Coy. CANTRAINNE — Refilling point for 138 Bryde. LE CORNET BOURDOIS — 453 Coy. LE REVEILLON — Refilling point for 137 Brigade. L'ABBAYE — 454 Coy. BAS RIEUX - Refilling point for 139 Brigade. OBLINGHEM near L'ABBAYE. Mr. of Supply Officers and Staff to here discussed 13th supplies to merge this from Brothers by Quarrymen officer 12th Conference to ensure 13th and Refreshments and Refreshments truck 13th	18510	324	S.99? R.1725	1274	✓

WAR DIARY
or
INTELLIGENCE SUMMARY.

(Erase heading not required.)

Army Form C. 2118.

Place	Date	Hour	Summary of Events and Information	All Ranks	S & AD	Animals R	L.D.	Mules	Remarks and references to Appendices
BUSNES	Apr. 13		Division moved to new area. Div. H.Q. from NORRENT FONTES to BUSNES - Units all Companies and Refilling Points in new area. Transferred to D.H.L. and others to Corps actions.	18241	311	R 938	1704	1219	2/81
	14		General experience of Supply and Transport arrangements. Special arrangements for ensuring rations and fuel by Lorries to Div Lethal and 1st Mounted Divisions then coming to new area. Refilling Point for Inf = 139 Bde-- HOUCHIN Divnl HQ cards of Brigade.	18328	311	R 921	1685	1219	2/81
	15		General experience of Supply and Transport arrangements. Units 2 new Companies and Supper Officers at Refilling points.	17243	312	R 1001	1669	1157	2/81
	16		Supply transport a front for new area - Refilling Point: -- 137 Bde LABEUVRIERE. 138 Bde LE HAMEL. 139 Bde HOUCHIN. Advd L'ECLEME.	16359	305	R 901	1653	1098	2/81
			DHQ Trucks LABEUVRIERE. Division moves to new area. Jourlike moved						
LABEUVRIERE	17		for new area 17th	15482	094	R 845	1636	1072	2/81
	18		LILLERS. Issued to 139 Bde Inf. Bn. DMO Chiefs. and Corps Balln 5th and 7th A.Bde and Derby Regt and 465 Coy R.E. and Mounted Details General experience of Supply arrangements	17049	300	R 932	1657	1132	2/81

Army Form C. 2118.

WAR DIARY
or
INTELLIGENCE SUMMARY.
(Erase heading not required.)

Instructions regarding War Diaries and Intelligence Summaries are contained in F. S. Regs., Part II. and the Staff Manual respectively. Title pages will be prepared in manuscript.

Place	Date	Hour	Summary of Events and Information	Strength - All Ranks	Strength - Animals S & HD	Strength - Animals LD	Strength - Animals Mules	Remarks and references to Appendices
LABOURRIERE	Apr. 19		General arrangements. Re arranged purchase power and supplies food in our area. Arranging to take over from D.D. 2nd Divn.	18249	311	R 959 1693	1218	
BRAQUEMONT	20		Refusing fresh supplies and fuel on hand. Drawn wood to cut up in camp delivery. General arrangements.	24701	482	R 962 3633	1765	
PAR NOEUX			Rations for today NOEUX. LES-MINES – Supply Column on at. Arrangements for rationing attached Divisional trains troops.			R 995		
LES MINES	21		General arrangements of supply arrangements. Refilling point 157 Bde.{Inf.} Bde. RUE DE SEBASTOPOL – 138 Bde.{Inf.} Bde. CHURCH BRAQUEMONT 159 Bde.{Inf.} Bde. RUE D'INKERMAN – ARTILLERY L'ECLEME.	25378	415	3578	2070	
	22		General arrangements of supply arrangements. German shells dropped about 6 Bde. or BRAQUEMONT in throughout L.H.ment. German shell hit Divn. and HdQrs. A for hits and wounded and hit no front camp done.	25758	419	R 977 3641	1990	
	23		General arrangements of supply arrangements. Letters + Others drafts and also General Ration. Supply Coln. Rem. g.	23926	603	R 961 3538	1924	
	24		General arrangements of supply arrangements.	25789	391	R 918 3447	2027	

1577 Wt.W10791/1773 500,000 1/15 D. D. & L. A.D.S.S./Forms/C. 2118.

WAR DIARY
or
INTELLIGENCE SUMMARY.

(Erase heading not required.)

Army Form C. 2118.

Place	Date	Hour	Summary of Events and Information	Strength					Remarks and references to Appendices
				All Ranks	S⁄s	HD	LD	Mules	
BRAQUEMONT	Apl 25		General supervision of supply arrangements. Units attached for rations from 2nd account – 8th Royal Sussex Regt – 3rd Section 2nd Co. R.E. – 118 L.F. Ad. Bde. R.F.A. – Mellow Bty – 193rd Co. R.E. – B Bty Special Bde. R.E. – 282 L.F. Air Bde. R.F.A. at Ventriculathieues, 241 10th Hors. 2nd 4th Durhams. "A" Battery 384 Bde. R.F.A. – 147th A.T.F. & Bde. R.F.A. "A" 79th Field Coy R.E. 5th Hafork Regt –	25252	417		R 892	2010	✓
NOEUX	26		General supervision of supply arrangements. Reported new distillery at Hd. 8 Man. Club – DISTILLERY BRAQUEMONT.	25277	421	3502	R 925	1995	✓
LES	27		Arrangements for erecting branch bookstalls issued for Divisions. Units as before with Personnel.	24709	401	2446	R 938	2000	✓
MINES	28		General supervision and arrangements for Pack supply.	22034	388	3352	R 940	1899	Braquemont Distillery opened today by Quarter Master.
	29		Visits of Inspection and distribution of Lunch to Drivers.						
	30		General supervision of supply arrangements.	21362	388	3256	R 946	1804	✓
	30		Lieuts N.f.Ck. and 7.9. Hall & Capt R.E. newly transferred. General supervision of supply arrangements. Capt. G.H Emory at Food	19341	363	3102	R 879	1672	✓

Signed [signature]

Confidential

War Diary

of

Senior Supply Officer

46th Division

1-5-17 — 31-5-17.

(Vol XXVI)

WAR DIARY or INTELLIGENCE SUMMARY

Army Form C. 2118.

(Erase heading not required.)

Instructions regarding War Diaries and Intelligence Summaries are contained in F. S. Regs., Part II. and the Staff Manual respectively. Title pages will be prepared in manuscript.

Place	Date	Hour	Summary of Events and Information	All Ranks	STRENGTH Animals				Remarks and references to Appendices
					S. & H.D.	L.D.	Mules		
BRAQUEMONT	May 1		General supervision of Supply services. Units detailed for Railhead - 3rd Aust. Divn. by 1st Bde A.R.Fd. 20. Cav Divn & Corps 6th 28th Bn A.R.F.d. 19th Bly R.E. Bly Spinkhard, 6th Infty Bde, 2nd Divisional Train 2nd Divl Ammn R. Bde 3rd Bde R.F.A. 2nd Inf Bde d. R.F.A.	22122	392	3260 R.939	1858	
NOEUX LES MINES	"	2	General supervision of supply services. Conference. Return to Divns. Corps and D.A.D.s visited. H.Q. Railhead and Refilling Points throughout the Lines of Commn Cake from 990. Drawn as required by Supply Column Base arrangement to Coal front Depot. FOUQUEREUIL drawn as required by Supply Columns. Wood from F.S.D. FORGE COLUMN Employment - STAFF Coal from Base - Road Sweeping Gun and Hospital improvements MechT. Eqp - Metalwork for Reserve Rations in supporting points.	22072	397	3273 R.943	1858	
"	"	3	Ditto	21889	392	R.3255 R.3278	1853	
"	"	4		21852	287	R.3357 R.3355	1860	
"	"	5		21673	287	R.3255 R.3317	1870	
"	"	6		21656	287	R.3441	1875	
"	"	7	(Braquemont closed) 7.15 pm (Braquemont opened) 8.45 pm	21745	387	R.3461 R.3520	1866	
"	"	8		22526	392	R.4311	1881	
"	"	9	Braquemont closed - Divn H.Q. damaged moved to HERSIN Accommodate.	21521	390	R.4148 R.4341	1884	
HERSIN	"	10		21290	357	R.4381	1836	
"	"	11		21063	450	R.4306	1950	
"	"	12		20512	441	R.4459	1900	
"	"	13		20595	433	R.4281	1921	
"	"	14		20853	438	R.4205	1908	
"	"	15		20484	449	R.4278	1904	
"	"	16		20530	441	R.4267	1905	

WAR DIARY
or
INTELLIGENCE SUMMARY.

(Erase heading not required.)

Army Form C. 2118.

Place	Date	Hour	Summary of Events and Information	Strength — All Ranks	Animals S&HD	Animals LD	Animals Mules	Remarks and references to Appendices
HERSIN	May 17		General supervision of supply arrangements	20068	438	4267	1905	
	18		Reconstruction of tram support rent. Army workshops in Béthune sheds extended and converted into dugouts by supply officers with 7000 slabs at LIÉVIN. M22 at H.25 dugs of Dam Store	20437	431	4273	1901	
	19		General supervision of supply arrangements	20395	429	4268	1905	
	20		"	20260	428	4264	1903	
	21		Units attached. 3rd division down Cy R.E. 114th A Bde R.F.A. 128 Labour Cy B.Cy Spencer R.E. 83 Labour Cy 415 divisional trains. 114 Bde R.F.A.	19247	425	3567	1697	
	22		General supervision of supply arrangements	19171	400	3570	1690	
	23		"	19220	396	3580	1695	
	24		"	19180	399	3576	1692	
	25		"	19321	398	3561	1694	
	26		"	19181	391	3552	1695	
	27		"	18908	396	3620	1695	
	28		"	18820	393	3579	1928	
	29			18849	398	3788	1685	
	30		On situation to commanding General Reserve & Division wrote submitting extra Canadian Brigade with this division sent to canteen and extra forage on a few hours notice from ration about certificate					
	31			18941	393	3607	1682	

Confidential

War Diary
of
S.S.O. 46th Divisional Train A.S.C.

From 1st June 1917 to 30th June 1917.

(Volume XXVII)

Confidential

Army Form C. 2118.

WAR DIARY
or
INTELLIGENCE SUMMARY.
(Erase heading not required.)

Instructions regarding War Diaries and Intelligence Summaries are contained in F.S. Regs., Part II. and the Staff Manual respectively. Title pages will be prepared in manuscript.

Place	Date	Hour	Summary of Events and Information	All Ranks	Strength – Animals S & H.D.	Strength – Animals L.D.	Mules	Remarks and references to Appendices
HERSIN	June 1		General supervision of supply arrangements	19150	392	3645	1681	
	2		Ditto	19309	392	3710	1683	
	3		Ditto	19116	391	3704	1683	
	4		Ditto	19149	391	3707	1679	
	5		Forwarded return of French coke manufacture showing consequent fuel understood	19036	392	3762	1678	
	6		General supervision of supply arrangements	18828	391	3693	1646	
	7		Ditto	18555	390	3684	1689	
	8		Ditto	18533	392	3703	1697	
	9		Return to D.D.S. of J. Div. Sup. Republic 330 "Operations etc	18689	392	3705	1702	
	10		D.H.Q. Correspondence, Rly Dept, Ry. Stay Points etc	18898	392	3728	1715	
	11		Arrangements for forage and press Supply. General supervision. General supervision and arrangements for forage etc. as allotted. Snow Haulers – Working parties &c.	18762	396	3712	1713	
	12		Ditto	19044	395	3715	1716	
	13		Ditto	19809	395	3709	1706	
	14		Ditto	20081	395	3721	1713	
	15		Ditto	18201	395	3722	1727	
	16		Ditto	18191	455	3723	1726	
	17		Ditto	18402	399	2561	1712	
	18		Ditto	18215	390	2689	1712	
	19		Ditto	18260	384	2664	1713	
	20		General supervision. Transferred our A.S.C. Brigade to 6th Div. SSO to expire. Clearing from estimate 10000 pieces for framewire	18427	384	3708	1706	

WAR DIARY
or
INTELLIGENCE SUMMARY.
(Erase heading not required.)

Army Form C. 2118.

Place	Date 1917	Hour	Summary of Events and Information	All Ranks	STRENGTH Animals S&MD	STRENGTH Animals AD	STRENGTH Animals Mules	Remarks and references to Appendices
HERSIN	June 22		General improvement of supply arrangements. Correspondence with D.A.Q. Railhead Refilling Point. Agreement of Rations	18639	384	2694	1705	
	23		Ration to each unit. Return to unit prior to D. Corps and S.O.S.	18506	384	2704	1704	
	24		Ditto. arrangements to attack date	20199	388	5250	1709	
	25		Ditto. Evacuation of Hush Plant Fever	18234	1105	4002	1591	
	26		Ditto.	19012	388	4849	1510	
	27		Ditto.	18765	386	3847	1509	
	28		Ditto.	18782	388	3882	1512	
	29		Ditto.	18791	399	3742	1509	
			Ditto.	18806	442	3849	1505	
	29		Conference 10.0.2.2. re delay of to the train of convoy on tortuous portion of the Ration and Ammunition. The use of Parkis transit modified accordingly					
	30		General improvement of supplies arrangements	18759	382	3845	1502	

Lt Col O.C. 46th Divn

TRENCH COOKERS

UNIT.	No of Trench Cookers issued for period :-					
	April 22/30.	May 1/7	May 8/14	May 15/21.	May 22/31.	
137th Inf.Bde.						) Fat returned
5th Sth.Staffs.	50	430	—	300.	800.	"A"
6th Sth.Staffs.	50	450	100	400	800.	) 1000 lbs
5th Nth Staffs.	50	50	200	100	850.	"B"
6th N.Staffs.	50	100	200	200.	400.	) 1391 lbs.
137th M.G.Coy.	—	—	—	20.	—	)
TOTALS	200.	1020.	500.	1020.	2850.	= 5590.
138th Inf.Bde.						) Fat returned
4th Lincolns.	130.	—	—	210	—	) "A"
5th Lincolns.	130.	115	—	160	180	1080 lbs
4th Leicesters.	130	—	—	90	—	"B"
5th Leicesters.	130	—	—	100	120	) 572 lbs.
138th M.G.Coy.	57	—	—	—	—	)
468 Coy.R.E.	33	—	—	—	—	)
TOTALS	610	115	—	560.	300	= 1585.
139th Inf.Bde.						) Fat returned
5th Notts.&.D.	50.	—	75	50.	—	"A"
6th N.& Derbys.	—	50	—	75	—	) 998 lbs
7th N.& Derbys.	50	—	75	50	50	"B"
8th N.& Derbys.	—	50	—	50	—	) 1293 lbs.
139th M.G.Coy.	20	—	20	—	20.	)
TOTALS.	120.	100	170	225	90.	= 705.
Divisional Troops						) Fat returned
NIL			NIL			) "A" 250 lbs.
						) "B" 235 lbs.

Total No. of Trench Cookers issued to 31st May. 7880.
Total No Manufactured.   "   "   8380.
Balance in Stock.   500.

Used in Manufacture of cookers		Underdrawals of fuel due to issue of Cookers	
Dripping "A"	2398 lbs.	Coal	28 tons.
" " "B"	1671 lbs.	Coke	20 tons.
Coal	1 Ton.	Charcoal	7½ "
Paraffin	76 galls		
Petrol	42 galls.		

Total fat received from Units:-		Used in making cookers		
		"A"	"B"	) = "A" 3388 lbs.
"A"	"B"	2398 lbs.	1671 lbs	) " "B" 3491 lbs
3388 lbs.	3491 lbs.	Returned to railhead.		)
		680 lbs	760 lbs	)
		Remaining in stock		)
		250 lbs	1060 lbs.	)

Major,
Senior Supply Officer,
46th Division.

Confidential

War Diary
of
Senior Supply Officer
46th Division

1-7-17 to 31-7-17

Volume XXVIII

WAR DIARY
or
INTELLIGENCE SUMMARY

Army Form C. 2118.

Place	Date 1917	Hour	Summary of Events and Information	All Ranks	S/HD	L.D	Riding	Mules	Remarks
HERSIN	July 1st		General supervision of supply arrangements	18418	405	2767	1068	1501	
	2		Areas for motor convoy west of divisional Trains area and Refilling Points - 137 Brigade ALLOUAGNE - 138th Brigade ORLENCOURT - MONCHY BRETON. 139 MAGNICOURT. Railhead and D.H.Q.	15041	271	2784	1066	1316	
	3		Moved from HERSIN and J. BATUS and Mule B.H.A. also Refilling Points and Rations. Brent Zone arrangements.	14520	270	2780	1065	1316	
	4			10678	232	650	461	609	
BATUS	5		Supply Stone are supply office for Infantry at 10 Div. New Siding recommend where to go to at 20 Div. Up to Div Railhead. Known by Mule to the British. Trains to Sharn Companies and suppose 44 hours and signed.	2730	116	1199	468	693	
	6			9725	241	552	454	676	
	7			2707	107	1189	473	667	
	8			9716	249	548	461	685	
	9		10 div.	2630	249	510	469	498	
	10		With.	10623	240	1123	473	681	
	11		Ditto	9730	106	553	478	697	
	12		Ditto	10548	256	588	456	680	
	13			10692	100	1146	458	696	
	14		General supervision of supply arrangements. Railheads and Train Convoys and Refilling Points. Obtained new ammunition and supplies to left of circumstance. 61 also 452 Company	10648	247	588	465	682	
	15			10672	243	548	452	679	
	16			5895	101	1166	464	696	
	17			11170	203	568	461	672	
	18			2665	100	1166	465	679	
	19		D.M.	10745	242	547	458	696	
	20			2863	239	1166	465	676	
	21			2676	100	548	457	677	
	22			9811	226	550	460	501	
	23			2660	100	1168	457	615	
	24			9968	226	598	456	504	
	25			2625	100	1167	456	504	

TRENCH COOKERS.

UNIT.	No. of Trench Cookers issued during period:-					
	July 1/7.	July 8/14.	July 15/21.	July 22/30.		
137th Inf. Brigade.						
5th South Staffs	400	300	300	300	)	
6th do.	300	100	100	300	)	Fat returned:-
5th North Staffs.	200	200	300	700	)	"A" "B"
6th do.	300	300	300	600	)	~~1000~~ lbs
M.G.Coy.	20	-	20	-	)	270 1075
1/1 Monmouths	-	-	-	200	)	
TOTALS	1220	900	1020	2100	= 5240	
138th Infantry Bde.						
4th Lincolns	-	-	100	-	)	
5th Lincolns	100	100	120	-	)	
4th Leicesters	-	250	50	-	)	"A" "B"
5th Leicesters	-	-	-	-	)	179 lbs 465 lbs.
T.M. Battery	-	25	-	-	)	
M.G.Coy.	-	-	-	36	)	
TOTALS	100	375	270	36	= 781	
139th Inf. Brigade:-						
5th Notts & Derbys	40	-	-	-	)	
6th do.	40	-	-	-	)	
7th do.	40	-	-	-	)	"A" "B"
8th do.	40	-	-	-	)	170 lbs 815 lbs
M.G.Coy.	20	-	-	-	)	
TOTALS	180	-	-	-	= 180	
Divisional Troops:-						"A" 10 lbs
178th M.G.Coy	-	-	50	-	= 50	"B" 265 lbs.

```
Trench Cookers carried forward from previous a/c ....... 500
Manufactured during period ending June 30th ............ 6391
                                                        6891
Issues during month ending June 30th ................... 6251
Balance handed over to 2nd Canadian Division ........... 640
```

	"A"	"B"
Total fat received from units	629 lbs	2620 lbs
Used in manufacture of cookers	409	2400
Balance to No.4 F.S.D.	220 lbs	220 lbs

Expended in manufacture   Saving of fuel effected
   of Cookers   by use of Trench Cookers

   Coal   5 cwts.   Coal   26½ tons
   Paraffin 73 galls.   Coke   53 tons
                                    C'Coal 12 tons

12th July 1917.

Major,

Army Form C. 2118.

WAR DIARY
or
INTELLIGENCE SUMMARY.
(Erase heading not required.)

Instructions regarding War Diaries and Intelligence Summaries are contained in F. S. Regs., Part II. and the Staff Manual respectively. Title pages will be prepared in manuscript.

Place	Date	Hour	Summary of Events and Information	\multicolumn{5}{c}{STRENGTH}	Remarks and references to Appendices
				All Ranks	\multicolumn{2}{c}{Animals}	Riding	Mules	
					S.& N.C.O	L.D.			
BAJUS	July 17		General supervision of Supply Services by Capt R. Coulmont	10407	225	526	452	617	(18th Div. Supp)
				2631	100	1162	456	504	
	18		Ditto	10452	225	521	452	617	
				2728	100	1200	451	504	
	19		Ditto	10141	224	560	459	621	
				2544	110	1310	475	505	
	20		Ditto	10201	224	551	459	620	
				2670	132	1280	482	505	
	21		Ditto	9929	224	540	459	618	
				2632	106	1276	464	499	
	22		Ditto	10149	224	552	459	629	
				2651	106	1277	463	507	
	23		Ditto	10848	224	568	457	660	
				2639	106	1269	462	503	
	24		Ditto	10821	225	567	450	660	
				2649	106	1275	452	502	
	25		Took over Capt. Coulmont. Must from BATUS.	16499	395	2818	452	1502	
	26		Turned OKQ Kriubes. Noney for Maier. Repairing points	2698	166	1273	462	502	
NOEUX LES MINES	26			16528	397	2830	1714	1528	
				2567	106	1272	462	498	
	27		Arrangement for these out trained purchases	18216	442	2805	487	1608	
				2545	106	1272	462	498	
	28		General supervision of Supply arrangements and reading	15914	277	2523	485	1459	
				2485	108	1271	469	503	
	29		ORQ General Conference and Supplies Officer	15016	279	2625	484	1489	
				2469	106	1269	460	502	
	30		New for to continuing suspertian of brood	16504	259	2707	482	1508	
				2474	112	1337	460	517	
	31		Carried forward supervision	16618	360	2705	476	1505	
				2508	176	1284	464	520	

A5834. Wt. W4973/M687 750,000 8/16 D. D. & L. Ltd. Forms/C.2118/13

Confidential

War Diary

of

Senior Supply Officer

46th Division

From 1st August 1917.
To 31st August 1917.

Volume XXIX

WAR DIARY or INTELLIGENCE SUMMARY

Army Form C. 2118.

(Erase heading not required.)

Instructions regarding War Diaries and Intelligence Summaries are contained in F.S. Regs., Part II. and the Staff Manual respectively. Title pages will be prepared in manuscript.

Place	Date	Hour	Summary of Events and Information	Strength - A/1 Ranks	Animals 3 HD.	Animals LD.	Riding	Riding Mules	Remarks and references to Appendices
NOEUX LES MINES	Aug 1st	1	General supervising of Supply arrangements. Returns to RAS.I	16756	398	3705	474	1501	
	2		Arrangements for to the further Field Punishment and Supply Officer	16783	399	3705	481	1500	
	3		Ditto	16558	404	3700	482	1502	
	4		Ditto	16583	406	3700	476	1500	
	5		Ditto	16745	394	3694	474	1500	
	6		Ditto	16711	396	4684	471	1500	
	7		Conference Div H.Q. Railways - Horse Companies etc.	16692	402	3688	471	1499	
	8		Ditto	16905	410	3684	463	1500	
	9		Ditto	16664	405	3686	468	1501	
	10		Ditto	16578	405	3688	468	1500	
	11		Endeavouring to obtain further scheme of Rabbit Skins	16539	399	3679	464	1497	
	12		Obtaining an estimate of amount fuel wood available in Divisional Area	16572	399	3670	467	1494	
	13		Conference - Div H.Q. Railways-Horse Companies	16610	395	3673	467	1489	
	14		Ditto	16545	380	3672	465	1489	
	15		Ditto	16525	397	3701	465	1489	
	16		Ditto	16736	399	3701	472	1489	
	17		Remained of 46th Divisional Train Journal experience. Commenced supplying Lucerne.	16450	399	3668	474	1489	

WAR DIARY or INTELLIGENCE SUMMARY.

Army Form C. 2118.

(Erase heading not required.)

Instructions regarding War Diaries and Intelligence Summaries are contained in F.S. Regs., Part II. and the Staff Manual respectively. Title pages will be prepared in manuscript.

Place	Date	Hour	Summary of Events and Information	Ranks	S. & WO	AM Animals LD	Riding Mules	Remarks and references to Appendices
NOEUX LES MINES	Aug 18		Commenced 46th Divisional Supply Services – Conferences. Periodical Supply Services – Conferences. Touring DHQ. Dumps. Conferences – Railheads and Refilling Points	15397	399	696	474 1490	
	19		Inspection of Refilling and Issuing points with A.D.S. & A.D.C. 46th Div. – Routine Inspection	15475	399	2679	475 1490	
	20		Ditto	15465	399	2661	468 1486	
	21		Ditto	15565	399	2659	473 1486	
	22		General Supervision of Transport and Supply Services	15654	399	2660	471 1483	
	23		Ditto	15777	398	2662	467 1479	
	24		Conference with 1st Capt. D.A. Corps and 46th Div. A.D. ranks with proposal of replenishments during the winter months	15720	398	2666	459 1479	
	25		General supervision of Transport and Supply Services	15732	372	2670	457 1476	
	26		Ditto	16076	370	2664	445 1475	
	27		Ditto	16044	370	2656	446 1476	
	28		46th Army pay now at issuing in Rations O.2.	15789	374	2650	442 1496	
	29		General supervision of Supply arrangements	15971	379	2662	432 1497	
	30		Ditto – Returning 6th and 46th Div. Supply	18280	484	2788	826 1731	
	31		Ditto	18220	484	2607	981 1755	

Confidential
War Diary
of
Senior Supply Officer
46th Division

1.9.17 to 30.9.17.

Volume XXX

Army Form C. 2118.

WAR DIARY
or
INTELLIGENCE SUMMARY.

(Erase heading not required.)

Instructions regarding War Diaries and Intelligence Summaries are contained in F.S. Regs., Part II. and the Staff Manual respectively. Title pages will be prepared in manuscript.

Place	Date	Hour	Summary of Events and Information	All Ranks	Strength Animals S & HD	A.D.	Riding	Mules	Remarks and references to Appendices
NOEUX LES MINES	Sept. 1		General supervision of Supply arrangements	18237	492	2817	877	1730	
	2		Correspondence. Relieving and Reliefs	18341	516	2817	877	1810	
	3		Routine. Refitting Bomb. Mortar Supply Officer attachments	18280	472	2854	895	1937	
	4		for 1st and 2nd Echelons. First Reinforcements Battalions to the 1st, 4th,	18614	511	2852	885	1929	
	5		2nd, 3rd, 6th and 6th Divisions	15230	348	1793	911	1154	
	6		General supervision of Supply arrangements	15150	354	1792	886	1155	
	7		Ditto	15078	350	1778	887	1139	
	8		Ditto	15119	356	1731	868	1165	
	9		Ditto	15410	356	1765	875	1153	
	10			15660	355	1745	871	1141	
	11			15493	354	1746	874	1152	
	12			15242	352	1744	871	1166	
	13			15082	351	1737	868	1156	
	14			15163	348	1735	867	1156	
	15			14948	348	1733	868	1174	
	16			14990	346	1732	865	1162	
	17		General supervision of Supply arrangements	15065	346	1725	867	1159	
	18		Ditto	15063	347	1694	874	1147	
	19			15073	347	1722	864	1156	
	20			15187	348	1693	865	1109	
	21			15463	346	1683	863	1205	
	22			15440	346	1684	851	1159	

Army Form C. 2118.

WAR DIARY
or
INTELLIGENCE SUMMARY.
(Erase heading not required.)

Instructions regarding War Diaries and Intelligence Summaries are contained in F. S. Regs., Part II. and the Staff Manual respectively. Title pages will be prepared in manuscript.

Place	Date	Hour	Summary of Events and Information	All Ranks	STRENGTH S&ND	Animals LD	Riding	Mules	Remarks and references to Appendices
NOEUX LES MINES	Sept.23		General supervision of Supply Services	15319	346	1678	867	1159	
	24		Ditto	15950	368	1972	866	1403	
	25			16107	368	1975	868	1402	
	26			15958	365	1994	867	1402	
	27		Handed over to Capt. R Qunhutered mint Serve on Special Leave.	15913	363	1968	874	1400	
	28			15935	364	1963	865	1298	
	29			16034	364	1963	865	1296	
	30			16195	364	1960	886	1295	

Confidential
War Diary
of
Senior Supply Officer
46th Division

1.10.17 — 31.10.17.

Volume 31.

WAR DIARY or INTELLIGENCE SUMMARY

Army Form C. 2118.

Place	Date 1917	Hour	Summary of Events and Information	All Ranks	S&WD	OR	Riding	Mules	Remarks
NOEUX LES MINES	Oct 1		General supervision of Supply Services by Capt. R. Donlinson OC 452 Coy. All moving any absence on Special Leave.	16087	362	1951	876	1396	
	2			16396	369	1944	876	1355	
	3			15979	369	1052	876	1395	
	4			16152	367	1956	872	1422	
	5			15872	369	1952	875	1390	
	6		Correspondence Abs. M.O. Reserves and Refilling Points. Local purchase arrangements. Suit Distributions &c.	15915	369	1948	874	1382	
	7		Ditto	15919	371	1940	872	1382	
	8		Ditto	16206	371	1942	869	1382	
	9		D.A.D.S. & T. towards Depôt & Supt. with D.A.D.M. 46th Divn	16502	371	1942	872	1382	
	10		General supervision of Supply arrangements	16203	372	1946	877	1381	
	11		Ditto	16496	372	1952	877	1382	
	12		Ditto	16690	372	1950	876	1385	
	13		Ditto	16628	372	1941	869	1384	
	14		Ditto	16456	372	1985	841	1385	
	15		Ditto	16593	385	2063	873	1373	
	16		Ditto	16632	367	2039	879	1371	
	17		Ditto	16647	373	2118	846	1374	

Army Form C. 2118.

WAR DIARY
or
INTELLIGENCE SUMMARY.
(Erase heading not required.)

Instructions regarding War Diaries and Intelligence Summaries are contained in F.S. Regs., Part II. and the Staff Manual respectively. Title pages will be prepared in manuscript.

Place	Date	Hour	Summary of Events and Information	All Ranks	Sq HD	LD	Animals Riding	Riding Mules	Remarks and references to Appendices
NOEUX LES MINES	Oct 18		General Supervision of Supply arrangements	16602	393	2193	877	1369	
	19		Ditto	16691	373	2190	881	1370	
	20		Ditto	17046	373	2269	880	1370	
	21		Ditto	17193	373	2269	894	1373	
	22		General Supervision and Record for O.E.O.	16930	401	2136	877	1421	
	23		Refs- Rulrs by Table Dremories Supplementaries no's 2 qts at W.3316. Lanrent Dement army form no 62 at W.3317. General Supervision of Supply arrangements	16882	391	2207	901	1372	
	24		Ditto	16996	388	2205	833	1388	
	25		Ditto	16692	383	2067	843	1363	
	26		Ditto	16678	383	2043	883	1360	
	27		Ditto	16727	383	2055	878	1356	
	28		Ditto	16969	381	2092	900	1356	
	29		Ditto	17381	356	2168	899	1378	
	30		Ditto	18120	336	3267	899	1395	
	31		Ditto	18159	302	3249	919	1391	

War Diary
of
Senior Supply Officer
46th Division

1.11.17. to 30.11.17

Volume XXXII

Army Form C. 2118.

WAR DIARY
or
INTELLIGENCE SUMMARY.

(Erase heading not required.)

Instructions regarding War Diaries and Intelligence Summaries are contained in F. S. Regs., Part II. and the Staff Manual respectively. Title pages will be prepared in manuscript.

Place	Date	Hour	Summary of Events and Information	\tSTRENGTH						Remarks and references to Appendices
				All Ranks	S & H.D.	L.D.	Cobs	h.Mules	S.Mules	
NOEUX LES MINES	Feb 1		General supervision of supply arrangements. Correspondence and office routine meeting requirements. Returns for D.A.S.T. Forage. Rations and Reports of panic. Returns for D.A.S.T. Forage. Rations. Vehicle Summaries. Supplies on hand. W. 3313. 3316. 331r. Leave to Church. Important Justine. Issue of wheels. Report. Issue or repayment of ... issue of ... and Oil to Divisions. Checking supply Officers Reports of ... and providing same to Record Press. Issue of personnel + supplies. Ration.	17412	412	2798		10255		
	2			17988	475	2785		14641	22	
	3		Ditto	17661	421	2716		14641	22	
	4		Ditto	17721	412	2893		12913	22	
	5		Ditto	17282	412	2830		12411	24	
	6		Ditto	17771	412	2813		12192	22	
	7		Ditto	17811	412	2700		14460	23	
	8		Ditto	17194	300	2716		1224	23	
	9			17242	302	2419		1221	23	
	10			17145	299	3411		1220	24	
	11			17037	291	3447		950	23	
	12			15059	226	1805	159	1073	24	
	13			16139	356	2633	63	1075	24	
	14		Ditto	16143	356	2519	66	1053	23	
	15			15172	251	2518	65	1053	23	
	16			16159	351	2588	69	1066	23	
	17			16050	350	2523	68	1056	22	
	18			16031	350	2713	69	1051	22	
	19			16043	350	2473	68	1049	23	

Army Form C. 2118.

WAR DIARY
or
INTELLIGENCE SUMMARY.
(Erase heading not required.)

Instructions regarding War Diaries and Intelligence Summaries are contained in F. S. Regs., Part II. and the Staff Manual respectively. Title pages will be prepared in manuscript.

Place	Date	Hour	Summary of Events and Information	Remarks and references to Appendices
NOEUX-LES MINES	Nov 20		General supervision of supply arrangements	
	21		Ditto	
	22		New Rly was opened at LABOURSE. Supply train arrived alongside platform which is designed into/onto portions for each Supply Officer, who each receives from the S.S.O. and staff the supplies and amounts to his consignment in waggons. A Discworth[?] his waggon[?] then always. The transferring staff are had proved to be entirely satisfactory[?] and in 4 hrs or so to come from the Supply Officers and NCOs to a point opposite[?] who then over the [illegible] of the supplies [illegible] for transfer orders at the [illegible] the arrangements for holding up liveries until up direct to brews on the Rys. [illegible] from the railhead.	
			General supervision of supply services Ditto Ditto Ditto	
LABOURSE	28			
	29			
	30			

STRENGTH

	All Ranks	S.A.D.	A.D.	Arrivals Coss	L.Mules	S.Mules	
	16082	350	2711	68	1050	22	
	16337	346	2702	68	1048	22	
	15955	347	2624	58	1047	22	
	16138	347	2566	68	1047	22	
	15361	347	2558	68	1047	22	
	16169	346	2549	68	1051	22	
	16256	346	2540	67	1045	22	
	16205	346	2558	67	1039	22	
	16217	346	2547	67	1045	22	
	16125	346	2541	67	1045	22	
	16658	348	2587	67	1046	22	

SECRET.

LIST OF UNITS RATIONED BY 46TH DIVISION SATURDAY, NOVEMBER 10TH, 1917.

H.Q., 137 Inf. Brigade. 137 Brigade Bomb School. 5th. South Staffs. 6th. do. 5th. North Staffs. 6th. do. 453 Co. A.S.C. 137 Bde. M.G.Co. 1/3rd. N.M.Field Ambulance 466 Field Co. R.E. Provl.Pioneer Batt. Depot	Refilling Point NOEUX LES MINES K.16.b.8.6.
H.Q., 138 Inf. Brigade. 4th. Lincolns. 5th. do. 4th. Leicesters 5th. do. 138 Bde M.G.Co. 452 Co. A.S.C. 468 Field Co. R.E. No. 8 Sanitary Section. 170 Tunnelling Co.R.E. No. 1 R.E. Workshop 1/1st. Monmouths. 138 Bde. T.M.B. No. 46 Supply Column.	Refilling Point NOEUX LES MINES K.16.b.8.7.
H.Q., 139 Inf. Brigade. 5th. Notts. and Derbys. 6th. do. 7th. do. 8th. do. 454 Co. A.S.C. 465 Field Co. R.E. 139 Bde. M.G.Co. do. T.M.B. 1/1st. N.M. Field Ambulance XXXXXXXXXXXXXXXXX "K"Co. Special Bde. R.E.	Refilling Point LABOURSE L.2.c.8.8.
230 Brigade R.F.A. 231 do. 232 do. 46th. D.A.C. do. s.a.a. section. H.Q., 46th. Divl. Artillery. 451 Co. A.S.C. 46th.D.H.Q.& Employment Co. 46th. Divl. Signal Co. R.E. H.Q., 46th. Divl. Engineers. D.A.D.O.S. 178 Machine Gun Co. I Corps Laundry. 1/1st. N.M., M.V.S. 46th. D.A. T.M.B's. H.Q., 46th. Divl. Train. Detachment M.M.P.	Refilling Point DROUVIN K.4.d.9.0.

Copy No. 1 to "G"
" 2 A.A. & Q.M.G.
" 3 D.A.Q.M.G.
" 4 A.D.M.S.
" 5 D.A.D.V.S.
" 6 D.A.D.O.S.
" 7 Div. Train.
" 8 }
" 9 } War Diary.

Copy No. 8

Major,
Senior Supply Officer,
46th. Division.

SECRET

War Diary
of
Senior Supply Officer
46th Division
1.12.17 to 31.12.17.

Volume XXXIII

WAR DIARY or INTELLIGENCE SUMMARY

Army Form C. 2118.

(Erase heading not required.)

Place	Date	Hour	Summary of Events and Information	All Ranks	S&HD	AD	Cooks	L.Mules	S.Mules	Remarks and references to Appendices
LABOURSE	Dec.1		General supervision of Supply Services	16100	349	2621	66	1038	30	
	2		" " " "	16050	349	2614	66	1038	30	
	3		" " " "	16104	349	2572	66	1037	31	
	4			16094	349	2569	73	1031	23	
	5			16131	349	2560	83	994	55	
	6			15865	349	2528	95	981	75	
	7			15963	349	2530	76	960	105	
	8			15901	345	2696	85	954	100	
	9			15902	345	2701	85	945	107	
	10			15831	345	2814	89	681	85	
	11			15113	345	2651	82	802	61	
	12		Return to D.D.S.&T. Army	15882	345	2601	91	794	39	
	13		General supervision of Supply Services	15841	342	2794	146	1006	30	
	14		"	15194	340	2454	148	998	36	
	15		Commenced 15th Dec. Issues	15964	358	2400	141	1063	26	
	16		General supervision of Transport	15696	354	2460	147	933	26	
	17		and Supply Services	15695	357	2413	150	930	26	
	18			15595	351	2460	152	959	25	
	19			16500	356	2451	151	989	36	
	20			15715	354	2475	150	991	26	
	21			15686	354	2458	149	955	26	
	22			15701	322	2461	151	949	27	
	23			15651	322	2409	150	933	34	
	24									

LIST OF UNITS RATIONED BY 46TH. DIVISION AT LABOURSE L.2.a.5.8.

137 Brigade H.Q.	139 Brigade H.Q.
137 Brigade Bomb School	5th. Notts & Derbys
5th. South Staffs.	6th. do.
6th. do.	7th. do.
5th. North Staffs.	8th. do.
6th. do.	454 Co. A.S.C.
453 Co. A.S.C.	465th. Field Co. R.E.
137 Machine Gun Co.	139 Machine Gun Co.
466th. Field Co. R.E.	1/1st. N.M.Field Ambulance
Brigade Pioneer Co.	"K"Co. Special Brigade R.E.
	139 Trench Mortar Battery
138 Brigade H.Q.	230 Brigade R.F.A.
4th. Lincolns	231 do.
5th. do.	46th. D.A.C.
4th. Leicesters	do. (s.a.a. section)
5th. do.	H.Q., 46th. Divisional Artillery
138 Trench Mortar Battery	451 Co. A.S.C.
452 Co. A.S.C.	H.Q., 46th. Division.
468th. Field Co. R.E.	46th. Divisional Signal Co. R.E.
No. 8 Sanitary Section	H.Q., 46th. Divisional Engineers
170 Tunnelling Co. R.E.	D.A.D.O.S.
No. 1 R.E.Workshop	178 Machine Gun Co.
1/1st. Monmouths	I Corps Laundry(BETHUNE SOUTH)
1/2nd. N.M.Field Ambulance	46th. D.A. T.M.B's
138 Machine Gun Co.	H.Q., 46th. Divisional Train
No. 46 Supply Column	R46 Post Office
	46th. Divisional Post Office
	1/1st. (N.M.) M.V.S.

Major,
Senior Supply Officer,
46th. Division.

December 10th. 1917.

Army Form C. 2118.

WAR DIARY
or
INTELLIGENCE SUMMARY.
(Erase heading not required.)

Instructions regarding War Diaries and Intelligence Summaries are contained in F. S. Regs., Part II. and the Staff Manual respectively. Title pages will be prepared in manuscript.

Place	Date 1917	Hour	Summary of Events and Information	STRENGTH						Remarks and references to Appendices
				All Ranks	S. AD.	LD	An.SAD	LD	A.Pkrs	S.mles
							Animals			
LABOURSE	Dec 25		General Supervision of Transport and Supply Services	15680	402	2476		151	990	37	App.1
"	26			15644	355	2474		155	988	37	App.2
"	27			15595	356	2471		154	993	37	App.3
"	28			16116	356	2476		155	994	27	App.4
"	29			15701	358	2519		161	1027	37	App.5
"	30			16202	355	2568		162	1059	37	App.6
"	31			15952	357	2573		165	1052	37	App.7

Arthur Moff
A.S.C.
it. Director.
Ao 6th Division

Confidential

War Diary
of
Senior Supply Officer
4th Division
from
January 1st. 1918
to
January 31st. 1918

Volume 35

Army Form C. 2118.

WAR DIARY
or
INTELLIGENCE SUMMARY.
(Erase heading not required.)

Instructions regarding War Diaries and Intelligence Summaries are contained in F. S. Regs., Part II. and the Staff Manual respectively. Title pages will be prepared in manuscript.

Place	Date	Hour	Summary of Events and Information	Remarks	STRENGTH					Remarks and references to Appendices
	1918					Animals				
					S.NO	LD	C.cls	L.Mules	R.Mules	
LABOURSE	Sept 1		General Improvement. Transport and supply	16120	356	2500	158	1049	140	See
	2		Inspection. Mules. Police afternoon. Officers	15942	350	2573	158	1047	40	"
	3			15061	357	2574	158	1047	40	"
	4		Inspection of Devonshire's	15915	356	2569	158	1043	39	"
	5			15172	356	2564	157	1042	39	"
	6		Inspection of M. Gs etc	15694	350	2563	158	1042	39	"
	7		Social inspection of Devonshire Division	15421	356	2556	158	1035	35	"
	8		Ditto	15513	354	2552	156	1032	39	"
	9		Ditto	15216	355	2548	155	1035	141	"
	10		Ditto	15239	356	2545	158	1034	39	"
	11		Social inspection of supply reserve	15244	356	2550	151	1026	39	"
	12		Ditto	15213	355	2560	155	1035	39	"
	13		Ditto	15111	356	2563	155	1025	39	"
	14		Ditto	15165	352	2566	156	1034	39	"
	15		Ditto	15412	352	2563	156	1021	39	"
	16		Also foundations 12th October. 11 Officers & hides	15412	355	2562	158	1039	39	"
	17		accompany 16th etc British refug. Board 930.	14820	353	2565	159	1034	39	"
	18		Corps P.Hup Bal 2300 class 400	14820	352	2573	155	1049	26	"
	19		1880 bob airplane from the first training 30	3184	64	292	31	120	18	Letters
			322 Before in Dr Poge ament company Brac	11758	250	2341	130	725	21	Indorse I
	20			3256	54	286	31	446	8	Letters
			General importance of supply organisation and	11722	283	2350	130	900	21	Indorsed
	21		transport to the referred from the review	8156	156	498	64	240	114	Checkins
			as Tellard shown environments	7977	216	2056	92	737	24	General

Army Form C. 2118.

WAR DIARY
or
INTELLIGENCE SUMMARY.
(Erase heading not required.)

Instructions regarding War Diaries and Intelligence Summaries are contained in F. S. Regs., Part II. and the Staff Manual respectively. Title pages will be prepared in manuscript.

Place	Date 1918	Hour	Summary of Events and Information	RANKS	S. AD	LD	OSS	briefs	briefs	Remarks and references to Appendices
INDOUSE	22		General supervision of supply arrangements	8834	158	554	64	930	140	INDOUSE
	23		Refund goods - 138 Bales Bobbins - 137 Bales Raw flax	7995	216	2054	22	758	211	INDOUSE
INDEURIEGE			General supervision of supply arrangements	11245	231	651	31	523	90	INDOUSE
			Reported return from ANNEZIN, 7 H. Q. moved to INDEURIEGE	2044						
	24		General supervision of supply arrangements	11494	254	950	120	568	38	INDOUSE
				2139	110	1306	31	331	—	INDOUSE
	25		Div. Conference at Den Priel, now at Det From	11080	244	950	118	647	33	KILLERS
			11th Div. Groups	2092	110	1500	31	331	—	INDOUSE
	26		Consolidation of units - R.P. for A. and I. C for R.E.	11125	248	2168	150	1036	38	INDOUSE
	27		General supervision of supply arrangements	13996	344	2460	1149	1040	365	
	28		Ditto	14051	342	2461	148	1044	35	
	29		Ditto	14416	336	2464	148	1043	35	
	30		Ditto	14852	334	2457	147	1076	35	
	31		General supervision of supply arrangements. Four Battalions referred to H.Q. for reinforcements. Dykkers - Return to D.A.I. and blotters	14806	334	2432	147	1037	35	

A 534. Wt. W4973/M687 750,000 8/16 D. D. & L. Ltd. Forms/C.2118/13

War Diary
of
Senior Supply Officer
46th Division

1.2.18 to 28.2.18

Volume XXXVI

WAR DIARY or INTELLIGENCE SUMMARY

Army Form C. 2118.

Place	Date 1918	Hour	Summary of Events and Information	STRENGTH							Remarks and references to Appendices
				All Ranks	S.A.A.	L.G.	Animals Rds	Picks	Shovels	
LABEUVRIÈRE	Feb 1		General Inspection of Leather Equipment	13900	330	21115	115	971	36	98
	2		Ditto	13820	332	22117	115	1362	36	98
	3		Ditto	13987	331	22111	1116	1036	36	98
	4		Ditto	13794	330	24334	1114	1032	36	98
	5		Ditto	13767	332	24251	1116	1029	36	98
	6		Ditto	13715	332	22125	1117	1019	36	98
	7		General Inspection – Returns and Reports of Units – Conferences – Returns Reports etc. all attended to							98
	8		General movement to area of Division – Moved over 231 Bde R.J.A.L.C. Div. 11th Divnl. train wag. & also 416 Coy. R.E. and 3 Companies of Hammock Enfanews on an H.Q and remainder 2 Companies Hammocks hand. carts supplied to I.O. 1st Corps troops. Detachments away now for rear front. Rifles Prints Dump 8th Corps 9th – 139th dump Prinein – 138th Bd dump Westrenem – 139 & bd dump	15323	352	2579	1116	1020	36	98
RUPIGNY	9		Hort Rieux – Div. Troops Gonnehem. Division moved accordingly to critical scheme. Dense 138th Bde. to Service Heureux of 139th Bde. 13th B.H.Q. and 139th Bde in reserve and moved. Rifles Prints Dump. 404 Lories 9th corps 104. 138th Inft. Bde dump. Genecours – 139th Bd dump assisted by H.Q units. Lairés – 137 Bd dump. Bns. Rieux Biv. Treh – R.A. units – Gonnehem. 452 and 454 Companies –	11893	324	1710	125	994	24	98

A 5834. W+W 4973/M 687 750,000 8/16 D. D. & L. Ltd. Forms/C.2118/13

Army Form C. 2118.

WAR DIARY or INTELLIGENCE SUMMARY.

(Erase heading not required.)

Instructions regarding War Diaries and Intelligence Summaries are contained in F.S. Regs., Part II. and the Staff Manual respectively. Title pages will be prepared in manuscript.

Place	Date 1916	Hour	Summary of Events and Information	Ranks	S&WO	L.D.	Animals R&M	L.Mules	S.Mules	Remarks and references to Appendices
RYPIAN	Feb 10		139 the Bde moved into new area - R.A moved to HQ at Repay - Repay Bouts - Divn HQ & reserve Bty. 139th Bde Group - PALFART - 138th Bde Group GOVEGAUE. 139th Bde Group BAINES - D. Dumps (R.A) HESTREM. 452 and 453 Coys Train returned from 13th Dumps - 451 and 454 Coys Train drew supplies direct from Railhead. General Supervisor - visited Railhead and R.P's.	11966	292	1756	125	1003	22	9/10
"	11		Ryday Bouts went for 10th receipt Dev Prospecto							9/10
			FONTAINE-LES-CROISILLES - Arrangements for Coal from Dist. Dumps BISNETTES and outskirts by W forces	11094	293A	1762	125	996	24	9/10
	12		General dispersion of supply arrangements - also conveyance to stabled & R.Hk and intercepts Issues	12105	267	1771	117	998	24	9/10
	13		also places for coup d' Janier. Coks-ge un Kackmes	12099	270	1751	122	1002	24	9/10
	14			12358	248	1815	122	1004	24	9/10
	15		Revised authorised supplement rates 2 Wh Oats	12399	242	1822	121	1101	24	9/10
	16		arrangements for feeding 139 Siamese Divnpresent arranged B.A.C Drew supplies from 11 R.B.D. 15 two charge spares	240 Indian						
			R.B. HEAD DIRT and arranged for 9 days Iron rats & take over to Advancement force I.L.D. Movement on 17th	12499	303	1802	121	1039	24	9/10
	17		General Supervision & troops movements - arrangements	145 Indian						
			pichal Vitales - Hopital Evenpancy	12462	304 Indian	1802	124	1094	141	9/10
	18		General Supervision and handing over to Captain M.	92 Indian						
			Dickerson	12332	304	1812	122	1033	24	9/10

Army Form C. 2118.

WAR DIARY
or
INTELLIGENCE SUMMARY.
(Erase heading not required.)

Instructions regarding War Diaries and Intelligence Summaries are contained in F.S. Regs., Part II. and the Staff Manual respectively. Title pages will be prepared in manuscript.

Place	Date 1918	Hour	Summary of Events and Information	Tanks	Strength S/Std	O.R.	Animals L.D.	O.S.	Vehicles L.M.Gs	Remarks and references to Appendices
Rupigny	Feb 19		General supervision. Repairing Arms, Rockets etc.	12432	304	1806	122	1032	23	RS
	" 20		Attended lecture on "Economy of Supplies" by Maj Gen Parker. R. Supplies at L.G.B. Set.	12157 12471	306 306	1807 1766	122 120	1032 1032	23 23	RS RS
	" 21		General Supervision. Repairing Arms & Rockets &c.							
	" 22		" "	12391	306	1766	120	1031	23	RS
	" 23		" "	12336	298	1742	123	1028	23	RS
	" 24		Took over 2301 Rhe. R.G.A. from 11th Division	12996	303	2391	144	1028	23	RS
	" 25		Returned to 25th unit. General supervision. Repairing Arms, Rockets etc.	10363 13119	305	2415	129	1029	nt	RS
	" 26		" "	12738	302	2265	128	1025	nt	RS
	" 27		" "	12895	305	2207	122	1027	nt	RS
	" 28		Repairing Arms of 137th & 138th Inf. Bdes. moved from HEUCHIN and COYECQUES respectively to AUCHY-AU-BOIS. 240th Supplement to 2 N.M. by horses to FOUQUIERES nod no dup rations.	12990	304	2419	128	1025	nt	RS

R. Robinson Capt
A/AA 46 Division

Confidential

War Diary
of
Senior Supply Officer,
46th Division
from
March 1st. 1918
to
March 31st. 1918

Volume XXXVII

Army Form C. 2118.

WAR DIARY
or
INTELLIGENCE SUMMARY.
(Erase heading not required.)

Instructions regarding War Diaries and Intelligence Summaries are contained in F.S. Regs., Part II. and the Staff Manual respectively. Title pages will be prepared in manuscript.

Place	Date 1918	Hour	Summary of Events and Information	ALL RANKS	STRENGTH ANIMALS S+RD / LD+LM / Cobs+SM	Remarks and references to Appendices
RUPIGNY.	March 1st		General supervision. Repairing Roads, Railhead etc.	12621	316 3496 132	R.E.
ANNEZIN.	2nd		Repairing Roads for 137th + 138th Rde. moved from AUCHY-AU-BOIS to BAS-RIEUX and ECQUEDECQUES respectively.	12924	323 3533 137	R.E.
do	3rd		Repairing front 138 Rde ECQUEDECQUES to BEUVRY.	13277	347 3560 176	R.E.
do	4th		137 " BAS-RIEUX to Distillery BETHUNE 137 " Du Gp HENCHIN to LEQUESNOY Road, and Dug Gp Repairs by 4 Km 3 a ST HILAIRE. North station. Gun Machine Gun conferences at ALLOUAGNE. formed with 26 M.G. Batn. amalgamated and formed with	13069	361 3507 137	R.E.
do	5th		Reached road LILLERS to CHOCQUES. Repairing Roads from LAIRES to DISTILLERY, and 189 Rde moves ST HILAIRE to ANNEZIN. No 1 Labour Bn. Du Gp. remain at AMMETTES, and supplies detach to lorry.	13103	273 3271 332	R.E.
do	6th		Repairing Roads 137 - 138 Rdes changed over from BEUVRY to DISTILLERY and vice versa. 1st Manouche taken on.	13266	360 3135 174	R.E.
do	7th		Arrived road R.O.S.T. to Annezin sent on to September kep.	14361	443 4321 174	R.E.
do	8th		Period 1st - 7th from Arthune. Repairing Roads Railhead etc. General Supervision.	14293	384 4205 173	R.E.

Army Form C. 2118.

WAR DIARY
or
INTELLIGENCE SUMMARY.
(Erase heading not required.)

Instructions regarding War Diaries and Intelligence Summaries are contained in F. S. Regs., Part II. and the Staff Manual respectively. Title pages will be prepared in manuscript.

Place	Date 1918	Hour	Summary of Events and Information	Strength All Ranks	Animals SYCD	EDGM Rh. SYM	Remarks and references to Appendices
ANNEZIN	March 9th		No further arrivals at BETHUNE dumps and made arrangements with Cave Office to draw by lorry from BRUAY. Drew for 9th, 10th & 11th to be drawn from 4th DAR instead of Railhead. General Supervision. Refilling dumps. Railhead etc.	17806	354	4205 173	RS
do	10th		"	18480	397	4215 173	RS
do	11th		"	14641	392	4189 180	RS
do	12th		Drew for period ending 11th drawn from BETHUNE.	15198	363	4197 182	RS
do	13th		468 2nd Li RS taken on from 11th Bn.	15797	362	4196 182	RS
do	14th		General Supervision. Refilling dumps. Railhead to.	15029	366	4216 18	RS
do	15th		"	15650	361	4258 180	RS
do	16th		"	17612	361	4254 187	RS
do	17th		Lewis School at BOMY closed.	16107	370	4234 182	RS
do	18th		General Supervision. Refilling dumps. Railhead to.	15896	359	4226 182	RS
do	19th		"	15847	360	4308 187	RS
do	20th		"	16498	362	4299 187	RS
do	21st		"	16511	366	4383 191	RS

Army Form C. 2118.

WAR DIARY
or
INTELLIGENCE SUMMARY.
(Erase heading not required.)

Instructions regarding War Diaries and Intelligence Summaries are contained in F. S. Regs., Part II. and the Staff Manual respectively. Title pages will be prepared in manuscript.

Place	Date 1918	Hour	Summary of Events and Information				Remarks and references to Appendices
				STRENGTH			
				ALL RANKS	ANIMALS		
					STHD.	LD+LM	M+SM
ANNEZIN	Aug 22		General Supervision. Rifle grens. Reduced to	16,477	863.	4432	186	R.S.
do	23		"	16303.	863.	4428.	173.	R.S.
do	24		Major Wade M.C. returned from leave and resumed duties.					
			R Bonhomme Capt					
do	25		General supervision. Rifle grens. Reduced Gas	15954	865	4329	177	
				888				
do	26		Do	15695	867	4442	177	
do	27		Do	15826	865	4350	178	
do	28		Do	16311	866	4401	198	
			Supply arrangements for new area	5431	863	4130	198	
			Good extent unsual weich been in from 11th M.G. Bn des	12,5142	479	5397	193	
BRACQUEMONT	30		Rifle Grens - Do. Dos for 138th Brigade at 139 Bedseiper					
	31	1:00	Same abundant "139 Brigade "138 Brigade in bivouac. General Supervision and arrangements for new forward area	22322	481	5266	173	
			Do	21211 959	479	5115	175	

Confidential

War Diary
of
Senior Supply Officer
46th Division
From
April 1st 1918
To
April 30th 1918
Volume XXXVIII

Army Form C. 2118.

WAR DIARY
or
INTELLIGENCE SUMMARY.
(Erase heading not required.)

Instructions regarding War Diaries and Intelligence Summaries are contained in F. S. Regs., Part II. and the Staff Manual respectively. Title pages will be prepared in manuscript.

Place	Date 1918	Hour	Summary of Events and Information	All Ranks	Strength Animals Saddled, L.V.	Loose, S.A.	Remarks and references to Appendices
BRUAY/MONTIGNY	1		General supervision of supply arrangements	21904	658	5022	171
	2		Correspondence – Return for D.M.A. and routine	2587	659	5286	176
	3		Rode to Mins- BOUVIGNY and Refilled Points Sqns – BOUVIGNY and CARENCY –	22461	426	5340	172
	4		Saw and inspected Points – attached to Second Guard Cav. and	24190	462	5227	139
	5		Saw and inspected Troop. attached to Div.	23119	449	5248	172
	6		Saw H.Staff in of M.S.Sqn. – went Div. – P.M. for	22958	445	5210	175
	7		Br. S.R. Major Arnott – Preparation to escort the Proposed ceremony	22624	442	5230	172
	8			18428 (minus)			
	9		To be required for ceremony	23247	484	5229	172
	10		Attended Cav. Div. (1 Sqn. attended) 1 Sqn. Arab bred Nam Cav –	22407	448	5249	167
	11		Rode to Timps and Local Purchase.	22135	458	5389	153
	12			22782	448	5299	160
	13		General supervision – Readjustment Rides	21443	396	5203	101
	14		Move from Bulgarians to BRUAY Report Public –	16522	321	2441	143
BRUAY	15		Div 2.5 fd. – BRUAY – 13th Brigade – HOUDAIN – 137th Brigade	16965	326	2469	—
	16			7502 (Indian)			
	17		MERSIN – 137th Brigade – HOUDAIN = Railhead HOUDAIN =	15015	311	3429	122
	18		Monthly courier arrangements for supply and	5466	209	2486	120
	19		additional requirements – 137th Brigade K.P. Ruits –	15585	317	2499	140
	20		General supervision of supply arrangements	16158	316	3512	140
	21		Last out of the arrangements – cheque Purchase	16282	339	3512	137
			Violin Review and Railway Dump	15902	322	3508	134
				1512 (Indian)			

Army Form C. 2118.

WAR DIARY
or
INTELLIGENCE SUMMARY.
(Erase heading not required.)

Instructions regarding War Diaries and Intelligence Summaries are contained in F. S. Regs., Part II. and the Staff Manual respectively. Title pages will be prepared in manuscript.

Place	Date 1918	Hour	Summary of Events and Information	STRENGTH					Remarks and references to Appendices
				All Ranks	Animals				
					S.y	HD & D	Mules Cobs	Sm	
BRAY	Apl 22		General Supervision and arrangements for moving	16071	331	3519		137	
"	23		and Refitting points in new area					137	
"	24		Moved to GOSNAY - field firing Points	15897	323	3510		137	
GOSNAY	25		arrangements for Church Parades for 26th	15966	341	3522		128	
"	26		Church Parades and Divl Band supplied	16269	325	3546		136	
"	27		Supervising arrangements on ranges, stables for horses	16205	340	3534		136	
"	28		Visited Ranges and Rifling Pits	16241	333	3456		136	
"	"			10315 (m.hass)					
"	29		Visited Ranges	16312	330	3462		136	
"	30		Arranged Kitchener Ranges and Rifling Pits	15057	331	3458		104	

A5834 Wt. W4973/M687 750,000 8/16 D. D. & L. Ltd. Forms/C.2118/13

Confidential.

War Diary
of
Senior Supply Officer
46th Division
from
June 1st 1918.
to
June 30th 1918.
Volume No. XXXX

CONFIDENTIAL.

WAR DIARY
OF
SENIOR SUPPLY OFFICER
46th. DIVISION.

FROM
MAY 1st. 1918.
TO
MAY 31st. 1918.

VOLUME. No. XXXIX

Army Form C. 2118.

WAR DIARY
or
INTELLIGENCE SUMMARY.
(Erase heading not required.)

Instructions regarding War Diaries and Intelligence Summaries are contained in F. S. Regs., Part II. and the Staff Manual respectively. Title pages will be prepared in manuscript.

Place	Date	Hour	Summary of Events and Information	Strength				Remarks and references to Appendices
				All Ranks	B. HD	Animals LD & 5M	Under 15	
OOSNAY	May 1		General Supervision of supply arrangements and Regimental duties.	15432	334	3462	134	
	2			15549	333	3468	132	
	3		Correspondence Scheme for D.O.L.I. 1st Army W.33/6. W.33/7. Ind. & Physical and Transportation Return to this dept. South to this dept. Pulse and Oats entitlement.	15501	332	3465	134	
	4			15204	333	3462	132	
	5		Events reported on hand, W.3513.	14505	282 (Indian)	3451	134	
	6			14802	321	3450	133	
	7		Arrangements for Horses to come to the depot of the Division for Cattle from overseas and	14801	325	3451	133	
	8			14742	322	3452	133	
	9		Remounts for Divisional Reserve of supplies. Ch.	14773	321	3421	135	
	10		Jud. bt not des. from Jaurefpies. Went there Cause	14687	325	3444	133	
	11			14497	321	342-	132	
	12		Beights efected of being fines	14906	312 (Indian)	3456	133	
	13		Transferred pts. are Jaurefpie = from Lourp	14795	317	3453	133	
	14			14752	310	3454	132	
	15			14867	310	3454	131	
	16		and output = the Cv. Lent. w/was Cote Burial	14799	310	3445	130	
	17			14795	316	3444	129	
	18			14727	315	3429	129	
	19			14741	316 (Indian)	3450	129	
	20		Ditto —	14656	317	3428	128	

Army Form C. 2118.

WAR DIARY
or
INTELLIGENCE SUMMARY.
(Erase heading not required.)

Instructions regarding War Diaries and Intelligence Summaries are contained in F. S. Regs., Part II. and the Staff Manual respectively. Title pages will be prepared in manuscript.

Place	Date	Hour	Summary of Events and Information		STRENGTH				Remarks and references to Appendices
				All Ranks	S. & WO	Animals 15H & over	Under 15H		
GOSNAY	May 23			14665	316	3424	128		
	24			14597	315	3415	128		
	25			14552	315	3422	128		
	26			13902	315	3418	127		
	27		Issued & received of supply arrangements	14137	316	3401	128		
	28		Minutes issued from BETHUNE area	13423	317	3408	128		
			Orders regarding & authority First Army	904					
	29		No. 56044/2 Q.A. d/ 13.4.18 & 21.4.18	13520	317	3394	130		
			Sick - 29412 hrs	13469	316	3400	128		
	30		Bethune - 2971 -	13519	320	3419	126		
	31		Lorck - 6125 -	13621	318	3422	128		
			Onward - 5100 -	13920	318	3426	129		

Army Form C. 2118.

WAR DIARY
or
INTELLIGENCE SUMMARY.

(Erase heading not required.)

Instructions regarding War Diaries and Intelligence Summaries are contained in F. S. Regs., Part II. and the Staff Manual respectively. Title pages will be prepared in manuscript.

Place	Date	Hour	Summary of Events and Information	Strength - All Ranks	Strength - S. & H.D.	Animals - LD & over 15½ hds	Animals - Under 15½ hds	Remarks and references to Appendices
GOSNAY	Jan 1		General supervision of supply and inspection	13797	318	3424	125	20/-
"	2		and Regimental Sections	13766	318	3428	128	20/-
"	3		Conferences - Visited daily Regimental Parks	936 (Indian)				20/-
"	4		Received - Dist. Col. Comdt. - Chiefs &c	14298	318	3413	128	20/-
"	5		D.19. Jan of Army - W.33.16. W.33.17. Offrs	14060	318	3423	128	20/-
"	6		Whites and others - Ammunition - Returns	14574	317	3414	128	20/-
"	7		Regimental - same to Adm Comdt. Petrol	14566	315	3416	128	20/-
"	8		and Oils for Divisions - Supplies on hand - W 33.15	14872	318	3424	128	20/-
"	9		Supplementary Army Corps requirements	15264	314	3420	128	20/-
"	10		Weekly strength states and G.703 to Division	14839	317	3426	128	20/-
"	11		Suppers and B.Q. Parcels - Returned	926 (Indian)				20/-
"	12		Arrangements for Divisional Reserve of Supplies	15327	317	3434	128	20/-
"	13		&c for military tour. Ch of Lime - Rum -	15308	313	3430	133	20/-
"	14		Whale Oil - Paraffin - Wick - Soda - Candles -	15421	318	3429	128	20/-
"	15		Solopas etched - and Chevril. Jam -	15544	315	3428	128	20/-
"	16		Arrangements for scale quickened and jam total.	15522	318	3428	128	20/-
"	17			15566	318	3431	128	20/-
"	18			15790	317	3428	126	20/-
"				928 (Indian)				
"				15222	317	3428	126	20/-
"			Fresh Cod, Lime, Oatmeal, Dubbins	15552	311	3424	127	20/-

WAR DIARY
or
INTELLIGENCE SUMMARY.

(Erase heading not required.)

Army Form C. 2118.

Place	Date 1918	Hour	Summary of Events and Information	All Ranks	STRENGTH Animals			Remarks and references to Appendices
					S & H.D.	L.D. & 15 hnds over	Under 15 hnds	
GOSNAY	June 19		General supervision of supply arrangements	16001	311	3426	127	App/1
"	20		Reinforcements for advanced and evacuated areas -	15739	309	3429	127	App/1
"	21		Forward and wastable areas -	15767	308	3432	127	App/1
"	22		1 Refugable from BETHUNE area -	15782	305	3419	127	App/1
"	23		Cottages - 7.15 # Feb 100 #	15532 913(Indian)	305	3414	127	App/1
"	24		As per Requisition Notes and return	15350	305	3409	127	App/1
"	25		attached then to Field Bakeries of Indians -	15478	305	3416	127	App/1
"	26			15465	305	3409	127	App/1
"	27			15496	304	3412	127	App/1
"	28		Issues of rations in store area in during month	15600	306	3414	127	App/1
"	29		after Reg'n Notes - 40850 kilos =	15482	304	3404	131	App/1
"	30			15537 872(Indian)	308	3407	132	App/1

Confidential

War Diary
of
Senior Supply Officer
44th Div.

1.7.1918 - 31.7.18.

Volume "4"

Army Form C. 2118.

WAR DIARY
or
INTELLIGENCE SUMMARY.
(Erase heading not required.)

Instructions regarding War Diaries and Intelligence Summaries are contained in F.S. Regs., Part II. and the Staff Manual respectively. Title pages will be prepared in manuscript.

Place	Date	Hour	Summary of Events and Information	Strength - All Ranks	Strength - Animals S & MD	Strength - Animals LD & other H'horses	Strength - under H'horses	Remarks and references to Appendices
GOSNAY	Jan 1st		General Supervision of supplying arrangements	15516	304	3384	131	97
"	2		to troops received – CAROHNE RICOUART on	15600	304	3442	132	97
"	3		Refilling points – HESDIGNEUL	15732	304	3441	132	97
"	4		Testing dairy ranches and refilling points, also	15519	304	3429	131	97
"	5		B2c. two D.P. issued trucks to bakery officers, and	15648	306	3432	131	97
"	6		Divisional Pack Dump –	15791	307	3429	131	97
"	7		Returns for A.D.S. and DG	15869	306	3432	131	97
			co 3318 to 3317	1107 (Indians)				
"	8		Summaries of supplies and found	15736	309	3429	131	97
"	9		Produces - Forms summary – Vegetable	15702	306	3423	131	97
"	10		Summary - Supplies on hand return - Pleat	15765	306	3443	134	97
"	11		and Oil item to Bde. Institutions Supplementary	15947	306	3455	134	97
"	12		Forage requirements of Railway 1st Division	15946	306	3450	134	97
"	13		Supplies undrawn during two months.	15935	310	3450	134	97
"	14		Eggs and slight return –	16008	321	3497	134	97
				990 (Indians)				
"	15		Statement for Br. Perichars and Div	16052	315	3484	134	97
"	16		D.G. – Forage and Forms of Divisious cases – Report sent	15985	318	3444	135	97
"	17		Semi autumn of Regt. ready up lastly was	16017	314	3448	131	97
"	18		with return to Director of Supply & Rqm	16382	315	3525	152	97

Army Form C. 2118.

WAR DIARY
or
INTELLIGENCE SUMMARY.
(Erase heading not required.)

Place	Date	Hour	Summary of Events and Information	All Ranks	S. & H.D.	Animals H.D.	Animals	Remarks and references to Appendices
GOSNAY	July 19		General inspection of troops in for Divisions	16359	315	3548	120	
"	20			16135	316	3559	121	
"	21			16048 1001	316 (Indians)	3550	124	
"	22		Ditto.	15961	316	3544	99	
"	23			16305	316	3531	123	
"	24			16319	316	3522	123	
"	25			16231	316	3522	132	
"	26			16222	314	3521	130	
"	27			16370	314	3523	124	
"	28			16225 1004	314 (Indians)	3522	132	
"	29			15945	313	3529	130	
"	30			16120	313	3521	130	
"	31			16253	312	3518	131	

Confidential

War Diary
of
Senior Supply Officer
46th Division

From
August 1st. 1918
to
August 31st. 1918

Volume XXXXII

WAR DIARY or INTELLIGENCE SUMMARY

Army Form C. 2118.

Place	Date	Hour	Summary of Events and Information	Strength Men	S.M.O./D.Draught	Animals L.Draught	Cobs	Remarks and references to Appendices
GOSNAY	Aug 1		General supervision of Supply Services	16190	313	3523	131	901
"	" 2		visited Railway and Refilling Points	16227	313	3522	131	901
"	" 3		Hospital Offices M.G. Coy and Brigades	16231	312	3518	129	901
"	" 4		Correspondence. Return - 5316 - 531? Cheshire	16366	317	3407	129	901
"	" 5		Summaries) Fuel and Vegetable Summary -	16519	312	3512	129	901
"	" 6			16640	310	3517	125	901
"	" 7		Conf. Summary. Same on Repayment	16142	311	3414	121	901
"	" 8		Issued to field Troops - W 3313 Inf & ad	16038	311	3456	121	901
"	" 9		Bonuses - Supplementary Conf Ry -	16214	311	3429	121	901
"	" 10		Petrol and Oil for Courrieres	16200	301	3428	121	901
"	" 11			16194 1360 (Indian)	301 (Indian)	3422	121	901
"	" 12		Drafted out Beer for units. Returns	16098	300	3417	121	901
"	" 13		Arrangements for Personnel Reserve Horses	16190	298	3413	120	901
"	" 14		held for emergency issue. Ch. of items -	15898	298	3412	120	901
"	" 15		Rum - Colonial Wine - M&R - Rum for down	15912	298	3410	120	901
"	" 16		Cecili. Issues for Alcohol - Cheval. Brns	15885	298	3408	120	901
"	" 17			15900	316	3411	120	901

Army Form C. 2118.

WAR DIARY
or
INTELLIGENCE SUMMARY.
(Erase heading not required.)

Instructions regarding War Diaries and Intelligence Summaries are contained in F.S. Regs., Part II. and the Staff Manual respectively. Title pages will be prepared in manuscript.

Place	Date	Hour	Summary of Events and Information	Strength - All Ranks	Strength - S/AD Indians	Strength - Animals Indians	Strength - Animals BMS	Remarks and references to Appendices
GOSHOP	Aug. 18		General supervision of supply services	15901	348 & 1008 (Indians)	3409	119	Apx
"	19		Arrangements for int. loss Col. Cheval	15821	320	3434	117	Apx
"	20		our Cul. purchases of Coy. Col.	15147	320	3429	116	Apx
"	21		Hands our setive duries line of Capt Wodar	15690	318	3430	117	Apx
"	22		General supervision of supplies service	15115	320	3428	116	Apx
"	23		Do	15465	319		116	Apx
"	24		Do	15347	321	3425	116	Apx
"	25		Do	15686	321	3422	116	Apx
"	26		Do	1019 (Indians)				
"	27		Do	15084	321	3423	115	Apx
"	28		Do	15145	321	3409	115	Apx
"	29		Do	15184	321	3418	115	Apx
"	29		Capt Ja Best handed over duties of S.S.O. to Capt. R. Jonkinson M.C. on 30/8/18.	15159	322	3423	115	Apx
"	30			15096	338	3406	115	Apx
"	31		Supervision of supplies &c	15125	337	3462	105	Apx

CONFIDENTIAL.

WAR DIARY
OF
SENIOR SUPPLY OFFICER.

46th. DIVISION.

From SEPTEMBER 1st. 1918
To SEPTEMBER 30th. 1918.

VOLUME No. 43.

WAR DIARY or INTELLIGENCE SUMMARY

Army Form C. 2118.

Place	Date	Hour	Summary of Events and Information	All Ranks	STRENGTH S & HD	Animals LD	Under	Remarks and references to Appendices
GOSNAY	Sept 1		General Inspection of Supply Services	15091	341	3461	117	
"	2		Do.	1018 (Indians)				
"	3		Do.	14592	359	3469	116	
"	4		Do.	15110	339	3462	115	
"	5		Do.	14669	339	3460	115	
"	6		Handed over to Major L.J. Wren	15711	339	3489	115	
"	7		General Inspection of Supply Services	15257	339	3486	115	
"	8		Return for R.10 Pars (?) 103618 103317 - 103513 103415	15262	349	3493	115	
			103398 - 103395. Supplies in hand - Sup. Coupe -	1018 (Indian)				
"	9		Cars Demand for CAHONNE - RICOURT	15266	337	3489	115	
"	10		Railhead ALLOUAGNE - R. Ts 139 Inf MARLES-LES-MINES - 13th Inf LOZINGHEN - 138 Inf L.T.S. MESDIGHEM	14846	361	3487	115	
"	11		Sept R. T. moved from GOSNAY. Moved over rail Aug	15086	339	3404	115	
	12		VERQUIN-FOUQUIERES Road via Inkwood Dump	15012	339	3450	116	
BEAUCOURT	13		Railhead 73rd CORBIE (SOMME) - R.Ts 139 REILLY -	14744	319	3437	114	
"	14		138 RIBEMONT - 139 FRANVILLERS - Dts BONNAY	14997	308	3434	114	
"	15			15477	318	3439	116	
"	16		General Inspection and arrangements for	15448	349	3461	120	
				1011 (Indian)				
"	17		Full Inspection Rawal Pc.	15361	346	3471	119	
				12096	247	1651	105	
				1935	129	1788	6	

WAR DIARY
or
INTELLIGENCE SUMMARY.

Army Form C. 2118.

Place	Date	Hour	Summary of Events and Information	STRENGTH				Remarks and references to Appendices
				All Ranks	Patients S.I.	L.D.		
Beauval	Sept 18		R.A. Units and 36 Coys - Refilled Point fumes	14905	361	2438	113	18/1
TERTRY	19		at TEMPLEUX-LA-FOSSE.					
			Beaumont and B.F. Units	12733	220	1685	112	Bse 18/1
			R.U. Units - WORMWOOD SCRUBBS	1929	84	1742	6	P.S.m 18/1
"	20		General Inspection of Supply	13048	220	1694	111	Bses 18/1
				1894	84	1757	6	P.S.m B 18/1
VRAIGNES	21		arrangements. Testing railhead	13088	260	1748	106	Bses 18/1
			R.U. Units WORMWOOD SCRUBBS	2082	84	1748	6	P.S.m B 18/1
"	22		and refilling trucks. Deputation	12698	254	1785	107	Bses 18/1
			of Local Soldiers Medal Ribbons					
"	23		arrangements for Divl Reserve and	874 (Indian)		1746	6	R.M. Units 18/1
			Reinforcements to Divs.	1988	84	1703	115	Bses 18/1
			Bo. Jnts. to PERONNE	12740	181	1744	6	R.A. Units 18/1
"	24		Bo. Jnts. to CARTIGNY	1976				
			R.U. Units WORMWOOD SCRUBBS	12838	251	1884	107	Bses 18/1
			Changed Refilled trucks and	1938	80	1757	6	R.A. Units 18/1
			stores in conjunction with					
"	25		R.U. Units - CARTIGNY	14631	210	2639	113	18/1
"	26		conformed to movements and	14563	208	2394	106	18/1
			Evacuation of Division,	182 (Indian)				
"	27		General Inspections	14250	292	3414	113	18/1
"	28		" "	14698	309	3439	112	18/1
"	29		" "	14143	305	3467	110	18/1
				1009 (Indian)				
"	30		" "	14135	304	3455	110	18/1

6th Divisional Train
A.A. & Q.M.G. 6th Division

CONFIDENTIAL

WAR DIARY
of
SENIOR SUPPLY OFFICER
46th Division

1/10/1918   to   30/10/1918.

Volume XLIV.

WAR DIARY or INTELLIGENCE SUMMARY

Army Form C. 2118.

Place	Date	Hour	Summary of Events and Information	All Ranks	By H.Q.	Animals	Drr as Rs renderd	Remarks and references to Appendices
In the Field	Oct 1		General exchanges of friendly services and exchange of distributions of Red X depots efficient. Runs cals any ordinary requirements	13992	306	3436	110	
	2			13311	308	3424	110	
	3			13076	312	3452	109	
	4			13466	311	3430	108	
	5			11469	320	3456	108	
	6			11466	319	3409	108	
	7		10th.	967 (Indian)				
	8		Worked extensively and received line over of Saturdine regions by thick	19194	318	3517	109	
	9			12212	320	3387	100	
	10		Now found friendly with supply arrangements to ourselves of Divisions went greater	12292	314	3410	100	
	11		at 21st	12422	341	3557	101	
	12		Indent on combination with French Commr	12290	325	3466	102	
	13		French Civilians found in village return	12761	289	3628	102	
	14		from the enemy	13395	334	3570	102	
	15		Lieutenant has inspected the entirety of	994 (Indian)				
	16		Medical comforts to Field Ambulances	13319	341	3527	108	
	17			14911	340	3421	107	
	18		General experiences, Rations -	13404	336	3493	107	
				13877	335	3289	107	
				14454	334	3435	106	
				706 (Indian)				

Army Form C. 2118.

WAR DIARY
or
INTELLIGENCE SUMMARY
(Erase heading not required.)

Instructions regarding War Diaries and Intelligence Summaries are contained in F. S. Regs., Part II. and the Staff Manual respectively. Title Pages will be prepared in manuscript.

Place	Date	Hour	Summary of Events and Information	All Ranks	Sy. WD.	Over 15hh	Under 15hh	Remarks and references to Appendices
Sulle field	Oct 19		General supervision of supply arrangements	13757	335	3495	106	
	20		Ditto	13476	330	3539	106	
	21		Countersign Return for W.O.L.	12866	330	3494	106	
	22		Ditto	12933	326	3679	116	
	23		General supervision of supply arrangements from 23/3/21	12862	326	3487	104	
	24		Countersign Return. Received Referred	12979	325	3467	111	
	25			13079 979 (Indian)	326	3470	105	
	26		Ponto y	13064	325	3359	101	
	27			13723	324	3358	101	
	28		Ditto	12920	324	3342	101	
	29			13055	323	3332	101	
	30		Arrangements for supply and transport.	12712	325	3328	101	
	31		Second sheaf of issues from FRESNOY to BOMAIN	13117	329	3362	979	

E. Sinnell
Lt. Col. Divnl. Tnsr.

Confidential.

War Diary
of
Senior Supply Officer.
46th DIVISION.

From November 1st 1918.
To November 30th 1918.

Volume No. 45.

War Diary or Intelligence Summary

Army Form C. 2118.

Place	Date 1918	Hour	Summary of Events and Information	All Ranks	Officers	Animals Over 15½	Under 15½	Remarks and references to Appendices
In the Field	Nov.1		General inspection of supplies available Railhead and Refying in touch with advance of Division	13152 961(Indian)	323	3385	94	20.
	2		and Refying in touch with advance of Division FRESNOY Railhead – BOHAIN	13485	344	3253	100	20.
	3			13518	294	3256	99	20.
	4		Ditto	13539	325	3591	99	20.
	5			13415	329	3595	100	20.
	6		Railhead – MONTIGNY FARM	14797	320	3588	99	20.
	7			14815	319	3696	100	25.
	8		Accounts and Returns for S.T. Army	14592	315	3762	102	27.
	9		General inspection – Correspondence Refitted points – Railhead fuel	960(Indian) 13620	326	3808	98	28.
	10		to denufectents and Refetation also FRESNOY 15 KPNOD Railhead VAUX - ANDIGNY	14701	329	3768	101	28.
	11		Reins, verifies stated data	14054	339	3482	102	26.
	12		Poudre Bones and Countehou Railhead	13820	333	3329	102	30.
	13		Cheval fund and Reservoir opho BOHAIN	14925	331	2764	102	24.
	14		General inspections - BELLICOURT	13982	322	3339	102	20.
	15		Ditto Railhead	13964 925(Indian)	322	3361	115	26.
	16		BOHAIN	12644	321	3281	109	20.

WAR DIARY or INTELLIGENCE SUMMARY

Army Form C. 2118.

Place	Date 1918	Hour	Summary of Events and Information	All Ranks	Officers	Animals HD. Over 15th	Under 15th	Remarks and references to Appendices
In the field from	18		General supervision of supply services Railhead BOHAIN	13339	330	3326	110	App 261
	19		Ditto	13530	320	3297	102	App 262
	20			13060	310	3242	103	App 263
	21			13614	305	3292	99	App 264
	22		Returned for A.T. duty	13084	204	3244	100	App 265
	23		General supervision	13282 841(Indian)	295	3252	95	App 266
	24		Ditto	13324	291	3268	93	App 267
	25			13801	293	3264	93	App 268
	26			13961	294	3258	93	App 269
	27			13844	295	3300	92	App 270
	28		Reached SOLESMES	14110	294	3299	93	App 271
	29			14248	294	3312	94	App 272
	30		Returned to duty	14299 820(Indian)	294	3295	94	App 273
				14125	295	3286	93	App 274

Original

Trans WR 43

War Diary
of
Senior Supply Officer
46th (N.M.) Division
Decr 1st – 31st 1915

Volume 46

WAR DIARY
or
INTELLIGENCE SUMMARY

Army Form C. 2118.

Place	Date	Hour	Summary of Events and Information	All Ranks	S, ID	Animals LD	Mules	Remarks and references to Appendices
Field	Dec 17			15724	252	2270	81	22/1
Force	18		General Supervision of Supply Services	15758	301	2255	81	22/1
	19		PPC	15722	301	2239	81	22/1
	20			14258 (SQN Indian)	301	2255	81	22/1
	21			13920	301	2224	81	22/1
	22		General Supervision of Transport and Supply Services. In command of PPC & 16 Divisional Train.	14010	302	2206	81	22/1
	23			12625	303	2211	79	22/1
	24			13137	297	2207	79	22/1
	25			12903	302	2015	78	22/1
	26			13025	297	2207	78	22/1
	27			13315	297 (Indian)	2207	78	22/1
	28			13337 (Indian)	299	2207	76	22/1
	29			13186	303	2248	96	22/1
	30			13026	300	2202	96	22/1
	31			13168	297	3224	96	22/1

16 Divisional Train

Greenwood

WAR DIARY or INTELLIGENCE SUMMARY

Army Form C. 2118.

(Erase heading not required.)

Place	Date	Hour	Summary of Events and Information		STRENGTH			Remarks and references to Appendices
				All Ranks	Animals S & M.D.	A.D.	Vehicles 6 S.W.	
India Peas	Dec 1 1919			14013	293	3285	93	101
	2			13981	293	3285	90	101
	3			14059	293	3281	90	101
	4			14299	293	3266	92	101
	5			15341	293	3260	90	99
	6			14528	293 (Indian)	3260	90	101
			General dispersion of supply services	905				
	7		are	14658	293	3253	98	98
	8		arrangements for Distribution of	16666	293	3255	93	98
	9		fuel and also for bulk issues are	15120	293	3253	90	100
	10			15042	292	3264	93	101
	11		G	16217	290	3263	93	99
	12		are reorganised. Supply columns	16022	295	3262	93	101
	13		are formed for army H.T.	15935	301	3249	94	101
				911 (Indian)				
	14			16045	295	3256	94	98
	15			16053	294	3253	94	96
	16			15940	292	3257	84	101

CONFIDENTIAL.

WAR DIARY

OF

SENIOR SUPPLY OFFICER

46th. DIVISION

FOR

MONTH OF JANUARY.

VOLUME No. 47.

Army Form C. 2118.

WAR DIARY
or
INTELLIGENCE SUMMARY

(Erase heading not required.)

Place	Date	Hour	Summary of Events and Information	Strength: All Ranks	Animals S. & H.D.	Animals L.D.	Cars %	Remarks and references to Appendices
In the field	Jan 16			12062	317	3090	95	App I
"	17			12878	323	3087	100	App II
				761 (Indian)				
"	18			12657	326	3032	97	App III
"	19			12585	321	3056	95	App IV
"	20			12563	320	3055	95	App V
"	21			12486	306	3030	100	App VI
"	22		General supervision of Supply Services	12426	307	3013	97	App VII
"	23			12160	310	2991	98	App VIII
"	24			12080	311	2984	94	App IX
				882 (Indian)				
"	25			12017	312	3040	96	App X
"	26			11915	308	2958	98	App XI
"	27			11930	308	2927	91	App XII
"	28			11878	308	2900	91	App XIII
"	29		General supervision of Supply Services	11899	305	2594	85	App XIV
"	30		Ditto	11829	302	2679	86	App
"	31		Ditto	11182	303	2640	83	App
				985 (Indian)				

Army Form C. 2118.

WAR DIARY
or
INTELLIGENCE SUMMARY

(Erase heading not required.)

Instructions regarding War Diaries and Intelligence Summaries are contained in F.S. Regs., Part II. and the Staff Manual respectively. Title Pages will be prepared in manuscript.

Place	Date 1919	Hour	Summary of Events and Information	All Ranks	STRENGTH Animals			Remarks and references to Appendices
					Sy HD	LD		
In the field	Jan 1		General Inspection of transport and vehicles carried out	13389	299	3176	96	WJ
	" 2			13159	299	3159	97	WJ
	" 3		Court No 6 Divisional Issues Orders Received J.L.	13200	298	3141	97	WJ
				842 (Indian)				
	" 4		SAULZOIR - Rifled Points - FRESNOY - LARDIERES - FONTAINE	13124	299	3166	101	WJ
	" 5		AU BOIS and BOUSIES - also visiting Coast	13046	302	3171	101	WJ
	" 6		Rifleing Points - 18th Corps transit from Recluses S.B.	13150	300	3165	104	WJ
	" 7		Horse Selection - Received forges M.T.	13038	302	3163	103	WJ
	" 8		General Inspection of M.T. lorries and Waggons	12916	291	3170	106	WJ
	" 9		Correspondent and Returns for Week - Arrangements for Bath	12876	302	3161	105	WJ
	" 10		Distribution when Room and Inflated.	12772	302	3156	105	WJ
			Hands in Report Board of Source D.S.O. & Bras	785 (Indian)				
	" 11			12915	300	3146	105	WJ
	" 12			12851	298	3104	98	WJ
	" 13		General Addresses of Subspc [illegible]	13128	300	3119	98	WJ
	" 14			13417	311	3118	99	WJ
	" 15		Received - LE CATEAU	13094	302	3103	95	WJ

2449. Wt. W14957/M90 750,000 1/16 J.B.C. & A. Forms/C.2118/12.

Confidential

War Diary
of
Senior Supply Officer
16th Division

From
1-2-19
to
28-2-19

Volume

WAR DIARY or INTELLIGENCE SUMMARY

Army Form C. 2118.

Place	Date	Hour	Summary of Events and Information	All Ranks	S & HD	I.D.	Cobsc	Remarks and references to Appendices
In the field	Feb. 1			11440	304	2501	82	
	2			11400	292	2464	80	
	3			11184	295	2408	78	
	4			10916	265	2491	80	
	5			10588	298	2492	79	
	6			10496	297	2486	79	
	7			10659	294	2490	76	
	8			10655 — Indian				
	9			10519	302	2529	76	
	10			9880	305	2462	73	
	11			10279	284	2409	48	
	12			9910.3	295	2401	45	
	13			9870	354	2382	48	
	14		General Supervision of Supply Services	9858	205	2365	55	
	15			9881 — Indian				
	16			9900	296	2401	76	
	17			9553	288	2438	74	
	18			8710	272	2308	63	
	19			9081	240	2272	71	
	20			8711	265	2168	60	
	21			8430	218	2102	68	
	22			8295	291	2043	65	
	23			860 — Indian				
	24			8420	294	2121	65	
	25			8397	302	2121	54	
	26			7772	303	2156	53	
	27			7770	303	2037	54	
	28			7831	298	2057	55	
	29			7414	300	2058	56	
	30			7434	303	2040	60	
	31			844 — Indian	302	1930	52	

Vol 48

Confidential

War Diary

of

46th Divisional Train R.A.S.C

From 1st March 1919.   To 31st March 1919

(Volume XLVIII.)

Confidential

War Diary
of
Senior Supply Officer
N6th Division

From
March 1st 1919
To
March 31st 1919

Volume XLVIII

Army Form C. 2118.

WAR DIARY
or
INTELLIGENCE SUMMARY

(Erase heading not required.)

Instructions regarding War Diaries and Intelligence Summaries are contained in F. S. Regs., Part II. and the Staff Manual respectively. Title Pages will be prepared in manuscript.

Place	Date 1918	Hour	Summary of Events and Information	STRENGTH	STRENGTH ANIMALS			Remarks and references to Appendices
				ALL RANKS	SHOES b H.D.	RIDING b L.D.	COBS b C.	
In the field	MAR. 1			7128	240	1933	43	
	2			10233	327	1855	53	
	3			5085	248	1703	43	
	4			6170	226	1725	32	
	5			6172	230	1665	46	
	6			5915	254	1574	51	
	7			5429	229	1508	40	
	8			827 — INDIANS				
	9			5642	239	1448	41	
	10			5428	226	1360	54	
	11			5251	229	1340	44	
	12			5258	241	1175	37	
	13			5305	228	1051	36	
	14			5262	209	948	30	
	15			5611	197	909	32	
	16			981 — INDIANS				
	17			5279	185	793	21	
	18			4328	124	778	23	
	19			5085	137	664	17	
	20			4906	135	647	17	
	21			4660	135	598	15	
	22			4607	130	587	4	
	23			4776	133	696	11	
	24			965 — INDIANS				
	25			4615	127	593	3	
	26			4672	132	601	13	
	27			4617	130	600	15	
	28			5382	130	598	15	
	29			4328	129	588	16	
	30			4468	100	553	12	
	31			4614	101	673	11	
				809 — INDIANS				
				4389	100	546	6	
				4296	99	550	4	
				4472	102	657	5	

General dispersion of Supply services

SENIOR SUPPLY OFFICER
========================

46th. Division
****

W A R   D I A R Y

Month of

M A Y   1 9 1 9
****

(Volume No. 51)

Army Form C, 2118.

WAR DIARY
or
INTELLIGENCE SUMMARY

(Erase heading not required.)

Instructions regarding War Diaries and Intelligence Summaries are contained in F. S. Regs., Part II. and the Staff Manual respectively. Title Pages will be prepared in manuscript.

Place	Date	Hour	Summary of Events and Information	Remarks and references to Appendices
Railhead CAUDRY	1919 May 1st			
	2			
	3			
	4			
	5			
	6			
	7			
	8			
	9			
	10			
	11			
	12			
	13		General supervision of Transport and Supply Services.	
	14			
	15			
	16			
	17			
	18			
	19			
	20			
	21			
	22			
	23			
	24			
	25			
	26			
	27			
LANDRECIES	28		Leave from 13th to 30th incl.	
	29			
	30			
	31			

DATE	STRENGTH All Ranks	Ships + M.D.	Riding L.D.
1919			
May 1st	2187	47	3
2	2158	47	3
3	2150	47	3
4	2122	47	3
5	2067	47	3
6	2056	47	3
7	2031	49	3
8	2010	49	3
9	2013	49	3
10	2124	49	3
11	1958	47	3
12	1952	49	3
13	1940	49	3
14	1823	47	3
15	1716	47	3
16	1763	47	3
17	1717	47	3
18	34232	94	3
19	-	-	4
20	-	-	4
21	3432	-	2
22	3410	94	1
23	-	-	1
24	3258	94	1
25	-	-	1
26	3201	94	1
27	-	-	1
28	3144	94	1
29	-	-	1
30	2758	94	1
31	-	-	1
Total.	56500	1454	62

www.ingramcontent.com/pod-product-compliance
Lightning Source LLC
Chambersburg PA
CBHW081355160426
43192CB00013B/2414